Document publié pour mieux faire comprendre aux
Canadiens la Charte des droits et libertés, et en souli-
gner l'importance dans leur vie de tous les jours.

Cette publication n'est pas un document légal. Les notes
dans cette brochure sont publiées à titre de renseignement et ne sont pas une interprétation légale des dispositions de la charte.

Vous pouvez obtenir d'autres exemplaires de cette publication en écrivant à :

Publications Canada
C.P. 1 986, succursale B
Ottawa (Canada)
K1P 6G6

© Ministre des Approvisionnements et Services Canada 1982

N° de cat. CP 45-24 / 1982-1

ISBN 0-662-51913-2

La Charte des droits et libertés

Guide à l'intention des Canadiens

Canada

Avant-propos

Lorsque les Canadiens des générations futures se souviendront de ce que nous avons accompli en 1981, je suis persuadé qu'ils seront fiers du nouveau chapitre que nous venons d'ajouter à l'histoire de notre pays.

Nous vivons actuellement des événements qui feront époque, car le Canada aura acquis grâce à eux sa majorité politique. Il aura franchi la dernière étape du long cheminement vers l'indépendance et la souveraineté qui commença en 1867, avec la création de la Confédération.

Ce cheminement fut parfois difficile. Mais à l'époque, les pères de la Confédération savaient qu'ils couraient d'énormes risques en jetant les bases d'un pays qui allait occuper toute la moitié septentrionale de l'Amérique du Nord. Au cours des années qui ont suivi, les Canadiens se sont montrés à la hauteur des défis et tout à fait capables de surmonter les obstacles que posait pareille entreprise.

Agissant aujourd'hui au nom de tous les Canadiens, le Parlement a pris les mesures nécessaires pour ramener la Constitution de notre pays à la place qui lui revient de droit, c'est-à-dire chez nous, au Canada. Cela signifie que nous n'aurons plus jamais à nous adresser au parlement d'un autre pays pour faire effectuer les changements que nous, Canadiens, voulons apporter à notre loi fondamentale.

La résolution parlementaire, qui définit le contenu de notre nouvelle Constitution et lui confère un caractère authentiquement canadien, est importante pour chacun de nous parce qu'elle consacre un grand nombre des dispositions qui constituent depuis longtemps les fondements de notre société et qui régissent nos activités.

Mais l'élément nouveau et probablement le plus important qu'elle introduit dans notre Constitution est la Charte canadienne des droits et libertés, car cette mesure touche les Canadiens dans leur vie de tous les jours.

Les droits et libertés garantis par cette Charte ne sont pas nécessairement nouveaux ou différents. En fait, les Canadiens sont portés à considérer la plupart d'entre eux comme des droits acquis de longue date. Ce qui importe, c'est que dorénavant ces droits et libertés seront protégés par notre Constitution et que les gens qui se sentent lésés dans leurs droits pourront en appeler devant les tribunaux.

Le long débat public qui a mené au rapatriement de la Constitution aura au moins prouvé que, pour les Canadiens, la garantie de leurs droits et libertés répond à un besoin tout autant qu'à un désir. Et l'enchâssement de ces droits dans notre Constitution marque en ce sens une étape décisive.

Il est possible que, dans l'avenir, nous voulions améliorer et perfectionner notre Charte des droits et libertés, pour accroître les garanties et les moyens de protection offerts à tous les citoyens du pays.

Une fois notre Constitution rapatriée chez nous, il nous sera possible d'effectuer ces changements comme nous l'entendons. Et nous le ferons en travaillant de concert avec tous les partenaires de la fédération, selon l'esprit qui a toujours animé ceux et celles qui, depuis plus d'un siècle, ont fait du Canada le pays d'abondance et de liberté qu'il est aujourd'hui.

Le premier ministre du Canada,
Pierre Elliott Trudeau

Préface

Dans une société libre et démocratique, il est important que les citoyens connaissent leurs droits et leurs libertés, et qu'ils sachent où obtenir aide et conseils dans le cas où leurs libertés sont lésées ou leurs droits enfreints. Dans un pays comme le Canada, vaste et varié, avec onze gouvernements, deux langues officielles et plusieurs groupes ethniques, la seule façon d'assurer une protection égale à tous est d'inscrire ces libertés et ces droits fondamentaux dans la Constitution.

Maintenant, pour la première fois, nous aurons une Charte canadienne des droits et libertés qui reconnaîtra à tous des droits, où que nous vivions au Canada.

Il est vrai que toute une panoplie de lois fédérales et provinciales ont garanti certaines libertés et certains droits fondamentaux. Cependant, ces lois variaient d'une province à l'autre et ainsi, les droits primordiaux n'étaient pas également protégés dans toutes les régions du pays. Maintenant que nos droits seront inscrits dans la Constitution, cela constituera un rappel constant à nos dirigeants qu'ils doivent exercer leur autorité avec prudence et sagesse.

En octobre 1980, le gouvernement du Canada déposait devant le Parlement une résolution concernant la Constitution du Canada et incluant une charte des droits et libertés. À la suite de débats à la Chambre des communes et au Sénat, un Comité mixte spécial formé de représentants des deux chambres était mis sur pied pour étudier la résolution.

Ce Comité a entendu quelque 300 témoins s'exprimant au nom d'environ 100 organismes de toutes les régions du Canada. Il a reçu en plus un grand nombre de mémoires contenant des suggestions constructives.

Le gouvernement du Canada a étudié avec beaucoup d'attention les mémoires et les témoignages oraux de tous ces témoins, tout en tenant compte des suggestions faites par les membres du Comité mixte spécial; et ainsi, 70 modifications importantes ont été apportées au projet de résolution.

Puis, le Parlement a entrepris de nouveaux débats et, en septembre 1981, la Cour suprême du Canada affirmait que le gouvernement et le Parlement du Canada agissaient légalement, sans toutefois être en accord avec les conventions constitutionnelles.

À la suite de cette décision, le premier ministre du Canada et les premiers ministres des provinces se sont présentés à la table des négociations en début novembre, et ils en sont venus au consensus tant recherché par les gouvernements canadiens depuis plusieurs décennies.

Cette publication vise à permettre aux Canadiens de mieux comprendre leur Charte des droits et libertés. Si vous avez besoin de renseignements supplémentaires ou si vous croyez que vos droits ont été enfreints, rappelez-vous que votre député fédéral et votre député provincial sont là pour vous aider. Plusieurs organismes fédéraux peuvent également vous venir en aide. On trouvera en fin de publication la liste de ces organismes et leurs adresses.

Le ministre de la Justice,
Jean Chrétien

Table des matières

Loi constitutionnelle de 1982*

PARTIE I
Charte canadienne des droits et libertés

Attendu que le Canada est fondé sur des principes qui reconnaissent la suprématie de Dieu et la primauté du droit :

Garantie des droits et libertés

Droits et
libertés au
Canada

1. La *Charte canadienne des droits et libertés* **garantit les droits et libertés qui y sont énoncés. Ils ne peuvent être restreints que par une règle de droit, dans des limites qui soient raisonnables et dont la justification puisse se démontrer dans le cadre d'une société libre et démocratique.**

« La mesure que je présente constitue le premier pas accompli par le Canada dans la voie de l'acceptation de la déclaration internationale des droits de l'homme ou des principes qui ont inspiré les auteurs de ce noble document. »

Le très honorable John G. Diefenbaker, *Déclaration canadienne des droits*, Chambre des communes, le 1er juillet 1960.

« Il ne peut y avoir de démarche plus sensée que celle d'inscrire dans notre Constitution les libertés et les droits fondamentaux que nous avons et qui nous sont chers. »

Le très honorable L.B. Pearson, *Le fédéralisme et l'avenir*, Ottawa, janvier 1968, introduction.

« Nous devons maintenant établir les principes de base, les valeurs et les croyances fondamentales qui nous unissent en tant que Canadiens, de sorte que par-delà nos loyautés régionales, nous partagions un style de vie et un système de valeurs qui nous rendent fiers de ce pays qui nous donne tant de liberté et une joie aussi immense. »

Le très honorable P.E. Trudeau, 1981.

---

* La résolution adoptée par le Parlement canadien en décembre 1981 fait mention de la *Loi constitutionnelle de 1981*. Une fois adoptée par le Parlement britannique, cette loi deviendra la *Loi constitutionnelle de 1982*.

Notes explicatives

Cette partie de la *Loi constitutionnelle de 1982* incorpore dans la Constitution la Charte canadienne des droits et libertés qui garantit à tous les Canadiens certaines libertés et certains droits fondamentaux essentiels au maintien de notre société libre et démocratique et à l'unité de notre pays.

Le gouvernement fédéral ainsi que les gouvernements provinciaux et territoriaux doivent respecter cette Charte qui protège :

- les libertés fondamentales
- les droits démocratiques
- le droit de s'établir et de gagner sa vie partout au Canada
- les garanties juridiques
- les droits à l'égalité pour tous
- les langues officielles du Canada
- les droits à l'instruction dans la langue de la minorité
- le patrimoine multiculturel du Canada
- les droits des peuples autochtones

Depuis bien des années, les Canadiens jouissent d'un bon nombre de ces libertés et de ces droits fondamentaux. Certains de ces droits ont été reconnus par la *Déclaration canadienne des droits* adoptée à l'instigation du premier ministre John Diefenbaker, en 1960, et par d'autres lois provinciales analogues. Mais en les inscrivant dans une Charte des droits faisant partie intégrante de la Constitution, on les précise davantage et on leur assure une meilleure protection.

Dans une société démocratique, les droits ne peuvent toutefois pas être absolus; il se peut qu'on doive circonscrire leur exercice à l'intérieur de certaines limites pour protéger les droits d'autrui. Par exemple, la liberté de parole doit être limitée par des lois sur la diffamation. C'est pourquoi cet article prévoit que les droits garantis par la Charte pourront être restreints par des règles de droit dont la justification puisse se démontrer dans le cadre d'une société libre et démocratique.

Libertés fondamentales

2. Chacun a les libertés fondamentales suivantes :
a) **liberté de conscience et de religion;**
b) **liberté de pensée, de croyance, d'opinion et d'expression, y compris la liberté de la presse et des autres moyens de communication;**
c) **liberté de réunion pacifique;**
d) **liberté d'association.**

« Comme de nombreux autres députés et Canadiens, je m'engage à ce que la Charte des droits soit inattaquable... »

Le très honorable Joe Clark, chef de l'opposition, Chambre des communes, le 23 février 1981.

Un autre type de restriction sera aussi possible à l'égard de certains droits contenus dans la Charte. Les libertés fondamentales, les garanties juridiques et les droits à l'égalité pourront faire l'objet d'une clause « nonobstant ». Ceci signifie que le Parlement ou les assemblées législatives provinciales pourront adopter des lois qui iront à l'encontre de certaines dispositions de la Charte, dans l'un de ces domaines. De telles lois seraient abrogées après cinq ans, à moins qu'elles ne soient expressément adoptées de nouveau. Ceci permettra aux élus du peuple, et non aux juges, d'avoir le dernier mot sur certaines grandes questions de politique. On sera ainsi en mesure de remédier à certaines situations imprévues sans avoir à procéder à une modification de la Constitution.

Cet article précise les libertés fondamentales que la Charte reconnaît à tous les Canadiens. Ce sont des libertés que la coutume et le droit ont rendu presque universelles dans ce pays. Désormais, ces libertés sont protégées par la Constitution.

Les Canadiens ont le droit d'aller à l'église de leur choix, ou de ne pas y aller du tout. La liberté d'expression, y compris celle de la presse et des autres moyens de communication, est garantie ainsi que la liberté de réunion pacifique et d'association.

Droits démocratiques

3. Tout citoyen canadien a le droit de vote et est éligible aux élections législatives fédérales ou provinciales.

Même si nos droits ont, pendant nombre d'années, été tenus pour acquis, il y a eu, au Canada, des cas où l'on a enfreint, par des mesures législatives, certains droits fondamentaux.

En 1937, par exemple, l'assemblée législative de l'Alberta adopta une loi qui aurait obligé les journaux à révéler la source de leurs nouvelles et à publier sans frais de l'« information » fournie par le gouvernement. En 1937, la loi du « cadenas » du gouvernement du Québec interdit la propagation du communisme et du bolchevisme en faisant fermer à clé les locaux utilisés à cette fin. Au début des années 1950, un règlement municipal adopté en vertu de la Charte de la ville de Québec interdit la distribution dans les rues de la ville de tout livre, brochure ou tract sans l'autorisation du chef de la police. Cet arrêté était une atteinte à la liberté d'expression et de religion des Témoins de Jehovah qui demeuraient à Québec.

Les droits démocratiques traditionnels sont tout particulièrement garantis par la Charte. Tout citoyen aura le droit constitutionnel de voter aux élections fédérales ou provinciales et d'être candidat à ces élections.

4. (1) Le mandat maximal de la Chambre des communes et des assemblées législatives est de cinq ans à compter de la date fixée pour le retour des brefs relatifs aux élections générales correspondantes.

(2) Le mandat de la Chambre des communes ou celui d'une assemblée législative peut être prolongé respectivement par le Parlement ou par la législature en question au-delà de cinq ans en cas de guerre, d'invasion ou d'insurrection, réelles ou appréhendées, pourvu que cette prolongation ne fasse pas l'objet d'une opposition exprimée par les voix de plus du tiers des députés de la Chambre des communes ou de l'assemblée législative.

5. Le Parlement et les législatures tiennent une séance au moins une fois tous les douze mois.

« *Toute assemblée législative peut demeurer en place aussi longtemps qu'elle le croit nécessaire. L'assemblée législative du Manitoba a prolongé son mandat de quelques mois en 1908. Celle de l'Ontario en a fait autant en 1918, jusqu'au retour des soldats d'outre-mer, puis en 1942 (pour un an), et de nouveau en 1943 (pour un an également). La Saskatchewan adopta une loi semblable en 1943 pour prolonger d'un an le mandat de l'assemblée législative, mais il y eut une vive opposition.* »

Le sénateur Eugene Forsey, Les Canadiens et leur système de gouvernement, *1979.*

Liberté de circulation et d'établissement

6. (1) Tout citoyen canadien a le droit de demeurer au Canada, d'y entrer ou d'en sortir.

Les seules restrictions au droit de vote et au droit de se porter candidat à des élections seront celles que l'on qualifie de raisonnables, telles que l'âge pour les mineurs, l'incapacité mentale, et certaines restrictions pour quelques fonctionnaires tels que les présidents d'élection dont le vote peut être déterminant. Il pourra par exemple y avoir certaines restrictions de se porter candidat pour les juges, en raison de la nature non partisane de leurs fonctions.

Selon un principe démocratique généralement accepté, un gouvernement ne peut garder indéfiniment les rênes du pouvoir sans solliciter un nouveau mandat des élec- teurs. Désormais, ce principe fera partie de la loi, dans un article de la Charte qui stipule que le mandat de la Chambre des communes ou d'une assemblée législative ne pourra dépasser cinq ans, sauf dans des circonstances exceptionnelles comme une guerre, une insurrection ou une invasion. Et même dans ce cas, la prolongation du mandat sera sujette à l'approbation des deux tiers des députés de la Chambre des communes ou de cette assemblée.

La Charte prévoit également que le Parlement et les législatures provinciales devront siéger au moins une fois tous les 12 mois. L'*A.A.N.B.* contenait une disposition à cet effet pour le Parlement fédéral, mais il n'existait jusqu'ici aucune règle semblable pour les assemblées provinciales.

Cet article prévoit que les Canadiens seront libres de demeurer au Canada, d'y entrer ou d'en sortir. La façon dont on a traité les Canadiens d'origine japonaise durant, et après, la Seconde Guerre mondiale illustre comment un gouvernement peut enfreindre la liberté de circulation et d'établissement. Au début des années

Liberté
d'établissement

(2) Tout citoyen canadien et toute personne ayant le statut de résident permanent au Canada ont le droit :
a) de se déplacer dans tout le pays et d'établir leur résidence dans toute province;
b) de gagner leur vie dans toute province.

Restriction

(3) Les droits mentionnés au paragraphe (2) sont subordonnés :
a) aux lois et usages d'application générale en vigueur dans une province donnée, s'ils n'établissent entre les personnes aucune distinction fondée principalement sur la province de résidence antérieure ou actuelle;
b) aux lois prévoyant de justes conditions de résidence en vue de l'obtention des services sociaux publics.

Programmes
de promotion
sociale

(4) Les paragraphes (2) et (3) n'ont pas pour objet d'interdire les lois, programmes ou activités destinés à améliorer, dans une province, la situation d'individus défavorisés socialement ou économiquement, si le taux d'emploi dans la province est inférieur à la moyenne nationale.

« ... Mais ici, nous formons un seul pays et nous sommes tous ensemble; et nous allons d'une province à l'autre comme nous allons d'un canton à un autre ou d'une ville à une autre... »

Sir John A. MacDonald, Chambre des communes, 1882.

« À ce propos, je trouve difficile de croire que l'inscription dans la Constitution du droit des citoyens à vivre et à travailler partout au Canada pourrait aller à l'encontre des intérêts légitimes des provinces. En fait, j'espère qu'un jour la libre circulation des services sera aussi mise hors d'atteinte des gouvernements. »

Le très honorable William Davis, premier ministre de l'Ontario, Conférence Financial Post, Toronto, le 26 février 1981.

1940, le Cabinet ordonnait, en vertu de la *Loi sur les mesures de guerre*, de leur retirer la citoyenneté canadienne.

De plus, cet article donne à tous les citoyens canadiens et à toute personne ayant le statut de résident permanent le droit de s'établir et de gagner leur vie partout au Canada. Depuis la création de la fédération en 1867, les Canadiens ont considéré ces droits comme acquis et s'en sont prévalus, mais jamais auparavant n'ont-ils été garantis par la Constitution.

La Charte garantit que vous pouvez vous rendre dans n'importe quelle province ou territoire, sans empêchement, et y chercher du travail. Vous pouvez aussi vivre dans une province et gagner votre vie dans une autre. Vous ne pouvez être soumis à des restrictions pour la simple raison que vous arrivez d'une autre partie du pays. Ceci n'empêche cependant pas les provinces d'imposer certaines conditions de résidence pour pouvoir bénéficier de leur services sociaux. En outre, les nouveaux arrivants seront régis, comme les habitants de longue date, par les lois et les usages d'application générale en matière de travail. Mentionnons par exemple les règlements relatifs aux qualifications professionnelles, à l'appartenance syndicale, à l'expérience, à l'état de santé, etc., à condition qu'ils s'appliquent uniformément aux habitants de la province et aux nouveaux arrivants.

Toutefois, les provinces dont le taux d'emploi est inférieur à la moyenne nationale ont le droit de mettre en œuvre des programmes de promotion sociale pour améliorer la situation des personnes défavorisées socialement ou économiquement.

Il est intéressant de signaler que les Canadiens se sont beaucoup déplacés au cours des dernières années. Durant l'année qui s'est écoulée entre octobre 1979 et septembre 1980, 421 854 personnes, soit deux pour cent de la population, ont changé de province.

Garanties juridiques

Vie, liberté
et sécurité

7. Chacun a droit à la vie, à la liberté et à la sécurité de sa personne; il ne peut être porté atteinte à ce droit qu'en conformité avec les principes de justice fondamentale.

Fouilles,
perquisitions
ou saisies

8. Chacun a droit à la protection contre les fouilles, les perquisitions ou les saisies abusives.

Détention ou
emprisonnement

9. Chacun a droit à la protection contre la détention ou l'emprisonnement arbitraires.

Arrestation
ou détention

10. Chacun a le droit, en cas d'arrestation ou de détention :
**   *a*) d'être informé dans les plus brefs délais des motifs de son arrestation ou de sa détention;**
**   *b*) d'avoir recours sans délai à l'assistance d'un avocat et d'être informé de ce droit;**
**   *c*) de faire contrôler, par *habeas corpus*, la légalité de sa détention et d'obtenir, le cas échéant, sa libération.**

« Notre société repose aussi sur le principe de la franchise, tant dans les tribunaux que dans les assemblées législatives, et sur une procédure équitable devant les institutions judiciaires, ce qui signifie, au moins, le droit d'être entendu et de présenter sa cause avant d'être jugé criminellement ou civilement responsable. Dans l'administration de la justice criminelle, on a offert des moyens de protection aux accusés, tels que la règle contre les confessions obtenues par la force, la présomption d'innocence et la protection contre les témoignages incriminant leur auteur. Ces protections n'ont pas une valeur absolue, mais leur diminution devrait être justifiée par les assemblées législatives ou les tribunaux. La Déclaration canadienne des droits, valable au niveau fédéral a reconnu ces valeurs, à défaut d'une reconnaissance constitutionnelle. »

Le très honorable Bora Laskin, juge en chef de la Cour suprême, Université de l'Alberta, le 4 mai 1972.

Ces articles énoncent les garanties juridiques fondamentales dont nous jouirons dans nos rapports avec l'État et avec le système judiciaire. Ces garanties visent à protéger toute personne et à lui assurer un traitement équitable lorsqu'elle aura affaire à la justice, et en particulier à la justice criminelle.

Ces garanties juridiques reprennent et élaborent celles de la *Déclaration canadienne des droits* de 1960, et la plupart font partie, depuis longtemps, des coutumes du Canada ou de ses lois ordinaires. En les inscrivant dans la Constitution, nous serons assurés que ni l'État ni les forces de l'ordre ne pourront nous en priver facilement.

Plus précisément, nous sommes assurés que le droit à la vie, à la liberté et à la sécurité de notre personne ne pourra nous être enlevé par les autorités, sauf en vertu de lois ou de mesures légales et justes.

Ces garanties juridiques interdisent également les fouilles, les perquisitions et les saisies abusives. En outre, même si la loi autorisant les fouilles, les perquisitions et les saisies est tout à fait raisonnable, on pourra contester la façon dont elles sont menées par la police; par exemple, la police ne pourra user sans raison de la force.

La Charte garantit également qu'une personne ne pourra être détenue ou emprisonnée arbitrairement. Un policier devra avoir des motifs raisonnables pour procéder à une arrestation.

Les droits relatifs à l'arrestation ou à la détention sont conçus pour vous protéger de toute action arbitraire ou illégale de la part des forces de l'ordre. Donc, toute personne arrêtée ou détenue aura le droit de connaître les motifs de son arrestation ou de sa détention, d'être informée de son droit d'avoir recours sans délai à l'assistance d'un avocat, et de faire contrôler promptement par un tribunal la légalité de sa détention.

Cet article reconnaît des garanties juridiques importantes à toute personne accusée d'une infraction à une loi fédérale ou provinciale.

11. Tout inculpé a le droit :

a) d'être informé sans délai anormal de l'infraction précise qu'on lui reproche;

b) d'être jugé dans un délai raisonnable;

c) de ne pas être contraint de témoigner contre lui-même dans toute poursuite intentée contre lui pour l'infraction qu'on lui reproche;

d) d'être présumé innocent tant qu'il n'est pas déclaré coupable, conformément à la loi, par un tribunal indépendant et impartial à l'issue d'un procès public et équitable;

e) de ne pas être privé sans juste cause d'une mise en liberté assortie d'un cautionnement raisonnable;

f) sauf s'il s'agit d'une infraction relevant de la justice militaire, de bénéficier d'un procès avec jury lorsque la peine maximale prévue pour l'infraction dont il est accusé est un emprisonnement de cinq ans ou une peine plus grave;

g) de ne pas être déclaré coupable en raison d'une action ou d'une omission qui, au moment où elle est survenue, ne constituait pas une infraction d'après le droit interne du Canada ou le droit international et n'avait pas de caractère criminel d'après les principes généraux de droit reconnus par l'ensemble des nations;

h) d'une part de ne pas être jugé de nouveau pour une infraction dont il a été définitivement acquitté, d'autre part de ne pas être jugé ni puni de nouveau pour une infraction dont il a été définitivement déclaré coupable et puni;

i) de bénéficier de la peine la moins sévère, lorsque la peine qui sanctionne l'infraction dont il est déclaré coupable est modifiée entre le moment de la perpétration de l'infraction et celui de la sentence.

12. Chacun a droit à la protection contre tous traitements ou peines cruels et inusités.

Tout d'abord, un inculpé devra être informé rapidement de l'infraction précise dont on l'accuse et devra être jugé dans un délai raisonnable. Il ne pourra non plus être forcé de témoigner à l'occasion de son propre procès. De plus, un inculpé ne pourra être privé sans juste cause d'une mise en liberté assortie d'un cautionnement raisonnable.

Cet article prévoit aussi que tout inculpé devra être présumé innocent tant qu'il n'aura pas été déclaré coupable, et qu'il aura le droit d'être jugé par un jury en cas d'infraction grave.

En outre, une personne ne pourra être déclarée coupable d'une action ou d'une omission qui, lorsqu'elle est survenue, ne constituait pas une infraction à la loi canadienne ou au droit international. Ceci empêchera l'État de créer des infractions rétroactivement.

Toute personne jugée et acquittée ne pourra être poursuivie de nouveau pour le même chef d'accusation. Si elle est déclarée coupable et est punie, elle ne pourra être jugée et punie de nouveau pour la même infraction.

Enfin, supposons qu'une nouvelle loi augmente l'amende ou la peine d'emprisonnement pour une infraction donnée. Tout inculpé ayant commis cette infraction avant cette nouvelle loi se verra alors infliger la peine la moins sévère.

Ces garanties prévoient que personne ne pourra être soumis à des traitements ou peines cruels et inusités; qu'un témoin aura le droit à ce qu'aucun témoignage incriminant qu'il donne ne soit utilisé contre lui dans d'autres procédures, sauf dans des cas exceptionnels comme le parjure; et, enfin, qu'une partie ou un témoin aura droit, dans toute procédure judiciaire civile ou criminelle, à l'assistance d'un interprète si cette personne ne comprend pas ou ne parle pas la langue en usage au cours de la procédure, ou si cette personne est sourde. Ce droit sera reconnu quelle que soit la langue employée.

14

Témoignage
incriminant

13. Chacun a droit à ce qu'aucun témoignage incriminant qu'il donne ne soit utilisé pour l'incriminer dans d'autres procédures, sauf lors de poursuites pour parjure ou pour témoignages contradictoires.

Interprète

14. La partie ou le témoin qui ne peuvent suivre les procédures, soit parce qu'ils ne comprennent pas ou ne parlent pas la langue employée, soit parce qu'ils sont atteints de surdité, ont droit à l'assistance d'un interprète.

Droits à l'égalité

Égalité devant
la loi, égalité
de bénéfice et
protection
égale de la loi

15. (1) La loi ne fait acception de personne et s'applique également à tous, et tous ont droit à la même protection et au même bénéfice de la loi, indépendamment de toute discrimination, notamment des discriminations fondées sur la race, l'origine nationale ou ethnique, la couleur, la religion, le sexe, l'âge ou les déficiences mentales ou physiques.

Programmes de
promotion sociale

(2) Le paragraphe (1) n'a pas pour effet d'interdire les lois, programmes ou activités destinés à améliorer la situation d'individus ou de groupes défavorisés, notamment du fait de leur race, de leur origine nationale ou ethnique, de leur couleur, de leur religion, de leur sexe, de leur âge ou de leurs déficiences mentales ou physiques.

« ... nous avons la possibilité d'édifier à l'intention de nos enfants et de nos petits-enfants un Canada encore meilleur que le Canada actuel — un Canada où l'égalité et la diversité iront de pair, où l'intérêt des plus faibles sera protégé ... un Canada qui, pour tout dire, servira d'exemple au reste du monde. »

L'honorable Jean Chrétien, Chambre des communes, le 17 février 1981.

C'est l'Association du Barreau canadien qui a demandé que l'article 13 soit modifié de façon à assurer une protection contre les témoignages incriminants tant aux témoins volontaires qu'à ceux qui sont obligés de témoigner.

Les droits à l'égalité que contient la Charte viendront s'ajouter aux dispositions antidiscriminatoires qui existent déjà dans les textes de lois fédérales et provinciales sur les droits de la personne. Cet article n'entrera en vigueur que trois ans après le rapatriement.

En vertu de la Constitution, tous les Canadiens, sans distinction de race, d'origine nationale ou ethnique, de couleur, de sexe ou d'âge, ainsi que ceux qui souffrent de déficiences mentales ou physiques, seront égaux devant la loi et auront droit à la même protection et au même bénéfice de la loi.

Pour la première fois dans l'histoire du Canada, la Constitution va énoncer de façon claire et nette que, pour les femmes, l'égalité n'est plus un droit à acquérir, mais que c'est un état de fait. La Charte assurera aux femmes une entière égalité devant la loi – non seulement une égalité de traitement dans l'application des lois, mais aussi une égalité dans leur contenu.

Toutefois, rien n'empêchera la mise en œuvre de programmes de promotion sociale conçus pour favoriser, entre autres, l'égalité d'accès à l'emploi pour les femmes.

Les handicapés ont tout particulièrement besoin d'être protégés contre la discrimination. La Charte permettra

« Je voudrais que cette résolution, spécialement la Charte des droits et libertés, figure dans toutes les classes de toutes les écoles de toutes les régions du Canada. Ce n'est pas que je crois à la propagande, mais plutôt que les constitutions traitent essentiellement des droits; que les droits concernent essentiellement les personnes; et que les personnes doivent être encouragées dès leur enfance à bien saisir le sens de leurs libertés propres, et à accorder encore plus de valeur aux libertés des autres. »

L'honorable Edward Broadbent, chef du Nouveau parti démocratique, Chambre des communes, le 20 novembre 1981.

Langues officielles du Canada

Langues officielles du Canada

16. (1) Le français et l'anglais sont les langues officielles du Canada; ils ont un statut et des droits et privilèges égaux quant à leur usage dans les institutions du Parlement et du gouvernement du Canada.

Langues officielles du Nouveau-Brunswick

(2) Le français et l'anglais sont les langues officielles du Nouveau-Brunswick; ils ont un statut et des droits et privilèges égaux quant à leur usage dans les institutions de la Législature et du gouvernement du Nouveau-Brunswick.

Progression vers l'égalité

(3) La présente charte ne limite pas le pouvoir du Parlement et des législatures de favoriser la progression vers l'égalité de statut ou d'usage du français et de l'anglais.

donc la création de programmes spécialement conçus pour améliorer les chances des handicapés, et elle assurera ainsi qu'on ne pourra remettre en question la validité de ces programmes.

La Charte autorisera également les programmes de promotion sociale destinés à améliorer le sort d'autres personnes ou groupes défavorisés qui auraient eu à souffrir de discrimination.

En dernier lieu, la liste des motifs pour lesquels il ne pourra pas y avoir de discrimination et celle des motifs justifiant des programmes de promotion sociale ne sont pas exhaustives. Ainsi, les tribunaux pourront déterminer de nouveaux motifs de non-discrimination là où les distinctions effectuées sont jugées inacceptables. Ceci permettra également la création de programmes de promotion sociale pour d'autres groupes de gens qui pourraient avoir été victimes, notamment de lois ou de mesures discriminatoires.

La Charte confirme que le français et l'anglais sont les deux langues officielles du Canada : cela signifie, entre autres, que vous avez le doit de communiquer en français ou en anglais avec l'administration fédérale et de recevoir les services dans la langue officielle de votre choix dans tous les cas où il existe une demande suffisante de services dans la langue en question. Vous avez aussi le droit d'utiliser l'une ou l'autre langue au Parlement et dans toutes les cours de justice relevant de la compétence fédérale. On doit noter que la Charte n'oblige aucun membre du public à devenir bilingue. Au contraire, elle garantit que les citoyens peuvent recevoir les services du gouvernement fédéral dans l'une ou l'autre des deux langues officielles, à leur choix.

Travaux du
Parlement

17. (**1**) Chacun a le droit d'employer le français ou l'anglais dans les débats et travaux du Parlement.

Travaux de la
Législature du
Nouveau-
Brunswick

(**2**) Chacun a le droit d'employer le français ou l'anglais dans les débats et travaux de la Législature du Nouveau-Brunswick.

Documents
parlementaires

18. (**1**) Les lois, les archives, les comptes rendus et les procès-verbaux du Parlement sont imprimés et publiés en français et en anglais, les deux versions des lois ayant également force de loi et celles des autres documents ayant même valeur.

Documents de la
Législature du
Nouveau-
Brunswick

(**2**) Les lois, les archives, les comptes rendus et les procès-verbaux de la Législature du Nouveau-Brunswick sont imprimés et publiés en français et en anglais, les deux versions des lois ayant également force de loi et celles des autres documents ayant même valeur.

Procédures devant
les tribunaux
établis par le
Parlement

19. (**1**) Chacun a le droit d'employer le français ou l'anglais dans toutes les affaires dont sont saisis les tribunaux établis par le Parlement et dans tous les actes de procédure qui en découlent.

Procédures devant
les tribunaux du
Nouveau-
Brunswick

(**2**) Chacun a le droit d'employer le français ou l'anglais dans toutes les affaires dont sont saisis les tribunaux du Nouveau-Brunswick et dans tous les actes de procédure qui en découlent.

Communications
entre les
administrés
et les institutions
fédérales

20. (**1**) Le public a, au Canada, droit à l'emploi du français ou de l'anglais pour communiquer avec le siège ou l'administration centrale des institutions du Parlement ou du gouvernement du Canada ou pour en recevoir les services; il a le même droit à l'égard de tout autre bureau de ces institutions là où, selon le cas :

a) l'emploi du français ou de l'anglais fait l'objet d'une demande importante;

b) l'emploi du français et de l'anglais se justifie par la vocation du bureau.

Communications
entre les
administrés
et les institutions du
Nouveau-
Brunswick

(**2**) Le public a, au Nouveau-Brunswick, droit à l'emploi du français ou de l'anglais pour communiquer avec tout bureau des institutions de la législature ou du gouvernement ou pour en recevoir les services.

La Charte reconnaît aussi le français et l'anglais comme les langues officielles du Nouveau-Brunswick, à la demande expresse de cette province. Les citoyens du Nouveau-Brunswick auront le droit, en vertu de la Constitution, d'utiliser le français ou l'anglais à l'assemblée législative, devant les tribunaux provinciaux et lorsqu'ils communiquent avec leur gouvernement provincial. Pour leur part, les citoyens du Québec et du Manitoba conservent le droit d'utiliser le français ou l'anglais à l'assemblée législative et dans les cours de justice de ces deux provinces. Ce droit a été reconnu au Québec par l'*A.A.N.B.* de 1867 et au Manitoba par la *Loi sur le Manitoba* de 1870.

Maintien en vigueur de certaines dispositions

21. Les articles 16 à 20 n'ont pas pour effet, en ce qui a trait à la langue française ou anglaise ou à ces deux langues, de porter atteinte aux droits, privilèges ou obligations qui existent ou sont maintenus aux termes d'une autre disposition de la Constitution du Canada.

Droits préservés

22. Les articles 16 à 20 n'ont pas pour effet de porter atteinte aux droits et privilèges, antérieurs ou postérieurs à l'entrée en vigueur de la présente charte et découlant de la loi ou de la coutume, des langues autres que le français ou l'anglais.

« *Le projet de charte protège aussi l'usage du français et de l'anglais. Je suis bien d'accord qu'une nouvelle constitution devrait préserver les droits et les obligations constitutionnels relatifs au français et à l'anglais.* »

Le très honorable J. Angus MacLean, premier ministre de l'Île-du-Prince-Édouard, devant le Comité mixte spécial, Ottawa, le 27 novembre 1980.

« *Les gens qui parlent français dans ce pays ne sont pas une minorité. C'est ce que déclare la* Loi sur les langues officielles *et c'est ce que je veux voir inscrit dans la Constitution. Ce sont des Canadiens qui revendiquent le droit de parler l'une des langues du Canada.* »

Le très honorable Richard Hatfield, premier ministre du Nouveau-Brunswick, devant le Comité mixte spécial, Ottawa, le 4 décembre 1980.

« *Je n'ai aucune objection à inscrire dans la Constitution les droits linguistiques des francophones et des anglophones. Le droit d'utiliser le français ou l'anglais, ou le droit de recevoir des services dans l'une ou l'autre de ces langues n'est pas, après tout, un droit que nous réclamons en tant qu'êtres humains. C'est une réalité essentielle du Canada, un élément essentiel de la Confédération, et comme tel, ce droit devrait évidemment faire partie de la Constitution.* »

Le très honorable Allan Blakeney, premier ministre de la Saskatchewan dans son mémoire au Comité mixte spécial, Ottawa, le 19 décembre 1980.

Droits à l'instruction dans la langue de la minorité

Langue d'instruction

23. (1) Les citoyens canadiens :
   ***a*) dont la première langue apprise et encore comprise est celle de la minorité francophone ou anglophone de la province où ils résident,**
   ***b*) qui ont reçu leur instruction, au niveau primaire, en français ou en anglais au Canada et qui résident dans une province où la langue dans laquelle ils ont reçu cette instruction est celle de la minorité francophone ou anglophone de la province,**
ont, dans l'un ou l'autre cas, le droit d'y faire instruire leurs enfants, aux niveaux primaire et secondaire, dans cette langue.

Continuité d'emploi de la langue d'instruction

(2) Les citoyens canadiens dont un enfant a reçu ou reçoit son instruction, au niveau primaire ou secondaire, en français ou en anglais au Canada ont le droit de faire instruire tous leurs enfants, aux niveaux primaire et secondaire, dans la langue de cette instruction.

Cet article de la Charte renferme des garanties importantes concernant les droits des minorités linguistiques, dans le domaine de l'éducation.

Les droits des Canadiens appartenant à la minorité de langue française ou de langue anglaise dans une province de faire instruire leurs enfants dans leur propre langue sont déterminés selon les trois critères suivants :

1. *La langue maternelle.* Si votre langue maternelle (la première langue apprise et encore comprise) est le français et si vous demeurez dans une province à majorité anglophone, vous aurez de par la Constitution le droit de faire instruire vos enfants en français. Ce critère est d'une importance primordiale pour les Canadiens francophones qui vivent à l'extérieur du Québec : en effet, il assure aux jeunes Canadiens-français la possibilité de recevoir leur instruction en français, même si leurs parents n'ont pas reçu la leur en français.

(3) Le droit reconnu aux citoyens canadiens par les paragraphes (1) et (2) de faire instruire leurs enfants, aux niveaux primaire et secondaire, dans la langue de la minorité francophone ou anglophone d'une province :

a) s'exerce partout dans la province où le nombre des enfants des citoyens qui ont ce droit est suffisant pour justifier à leur endroit la prestation, sur les fonds publics, de l'instruction dans la langue de la minorité;

b) comprend, lorsque le nombre de ces enfants le justifie, le droit de les faire instruire dans des établissements d'enseignement de la minorité linguistique financés sur les fonds publics.

Entrée en
vigueur de
l'alinéa 23(1)a)
pour le Québec

59. (1) L'alinéa 23(1)a) entre en vigueur pour le Québec à la date fixée par proclamation de la Reine ou du gouverneur général sous le grand sceau du Canada.

(2) La proclamation visée au paragraphe (1) ne peut être prise qu'après autorisation de l'assemblée législative ou du gouvernement du Québec.

(3) Le présent article peut être abrogé à la date d'entrée en vigueur de l'alinéa 23(1)a) pour le Québec, et la présente loi faire l'objet, dès cette abrogation, des modifications et changements de numérotation qui en découlent, par proclamation de la Reine ou du gouverneur général sous le grand sceau du Canada.*

---

* L'article 59 de la *Loi constitutionnelle de 1982* ne fait pas partie de la Charte des droits et libertés. Il est toutefois reproduit ici parce qu'il se rapporte directement à la question des droits à l'instruction dans la langue de la minorité.

2. *La langue d'instruction des parents (au Canada).* Si vous avez reçu votre instruction en anglais au Canada et si vous vivez au Québec, vous pouvez envoyer vos enfants dans une école anglaise dans cette province. De la même façon, si vous avez reçu votre instruction en français au Canada et si vous vivez dans une des neuf provinces à majorité anglophone, vos enfants peuvent recevoir leur instruction en français dans ces provinces.

3. *La langue d'instruction des autres enfants de la famille.* Si l'un de vos enfants a reçu ou reçoit son instruction primaire ou secondaire en français ou en anglais au Canada, vous avez le droit de faire instruire vos autres enfants dans la même langue.

Ces trois critères sont soumis à la condition qu'il y ait assez d'enfants dans une région donnée, appartenant à une même minorité linguistique, pour justifier à leur endroit la prestation, à même les fonds publics, de l'instruction dans la langue de cette minorité.

Les deuxième et troisième critères, c'est-à-dire la langue d'instruction des parents et des autres enfants de la famille, s'appliquent aux systèmes d'éducation dans la langue de la minorité (que ce soit le français ou l'anglais) dans chacune des dix provinces. Lorsqu'une personne peut satisfaire à l'un ou l'autre de ces critères, elle jouit d'un droit garanti par la Constitution à l'accès aux systèmes d'éducation dans la langue de la minorité linguistique et ceci à travers tout le Canada.

Le premier critère, la langue maternelle, est en vigueur dans toutes les provinces, sauf le Québec.

Afin de tenir compte des désirs du Québec, la résolution constitutionnelle contient une clause particulière au sujet de l'application dans cette province du critère de la langue maternelle (article 23(1)a). Ce critère ne s'appliquera pas au Québec à moins que son emploi ne soit autorisé au préalable par l'assemblée législative ou le gouvernement du Québec.

« Je pense que nous sommes d'accord avec l'idée qu'on doit avoir une charte des droits dans la Constitution, c'est quelque chose que nous avons proposé depuis longtemps; et, finalement, je pense que la question des droits linguistiques, l'idée de M. Trudeau de garantir les droits minoritaires linguistiques dans l'enseignement à travers le Canada, c'est quelque chose qu'on doit faire et qu'on doit faire vite. Monsieur Trudeau a travaillé pour ça courageusement depuis maintenant 15 ans et, comme vous le savez, nous sommes complètement d'accord. En effet, y a du bon dans ce texte. »

M. Robert Bourassa, ancien premier ministre du Québec, Radio-Québec, le 2 novembre 1980.

Recours

Recours en cas d'atteinte aux droits et libertés

24. (1) Toute personne, victime de violation ou de négation des droits ou libertés qui lui sont garantis par la présente charte, peut s'adresser à un tribunal compétent pour obtenir la réparation que le tribunal estime convenable et juste eu égard aux circonstances.

Irrecevabilité d'éléments de preuve qui risqueraient de déconsidérer l'administration de la justice

(2) Lorsque, dans une instance visée au paragraphe (1), le tribunal a conclu que des éléments de preuve ont été obtenus dans des conditions qui portent atteinte aux droits ou libertés garantis par la présente charte, ces éléments de preuve sont écartés s'il est établi, eu égard aux circonstances, que leur utilisation est susceptible de déconsidérer l'administration de la justice.

Jusqu'à ce que cette autorisation soit donnée, seuls les citoyens qui ont reçu leur instruction en anglais au Canada ou qui ont des enfants qui reçoivent leur instruction en anglais au Canada jouissent d'un droit constitutionnel de faire instruire tous leurs enfants en anglais au Québec.

Cet article de la Charte prévoit que toute personne qui estime que ses droits ont été lésés, soit par une loi, soit par une action de l'État, peut s'adresser à un tribunal pour obtenir, selon les circonstances, une juste réparation.

Les exemples suivants feront mieux comprendre les cas où l'on pourra avoir recours à cette disposition de la Charte. Si un fonctionnaire essayait d'empêcher votre groupe de pratiquer sa religion, vous pourriez demander une ordonnance de la cour l'empêchant d'agir ainsi; vous pourriez aussi demander des dommages-intérêts, selon le cas. Une personne inculpée qui se verrait refuser une mise en liberté sous cautionnement sans juste raison pourrait présenter sa cause à un autre tribunal. Si la police obtenait des éléments de preuve en effectuant des fouilles qu'un tribunal jugerait abusives, le tribunal pourrait refuser d'accepter cette preuve à l'occasion d'un procès au cours duquel il serait allégué que l'on a enfreint un droit garanti par la Charte, et reconnu que

Dispositions générales

Maintien des droits
et libertés des
autochtones

25. Le fait que la présente charte garantit certains droits et libertés ne porte pas atteinte aux droits ou libertés — ancestraux, issus de traités ou autres — des peuples autochtones du Canada, notamment :

a) **aux droits ou libertés reconnus par la Proclamation royale du 7 octobre 1763;**

b) **aux droits ou libertés acquis par règlement de revendications territoriales.**

l'utilisation de cette preuve déconsidère l'exercice de la justice. Ce pouvoir de refuser certains éléments de preuve dans des circonstances précises va aider à maintenir le respect du public pour le système judiciaire.

La question très importante des droits des peuples autochtones du Canada, soit les Métis, les Indiens ou les Inuit, fait l'objet de plusieurs dispositions de la Charte canadienne des droits et libertés, de même que de la nouvelle Constitution.

À la demande expresse de certains groupes autochtones, des dispositions spéciales ont été insérées dans la Constitution. Les représentants de ces groupes ont fait valoir avec vigueur la nécessité de reconnaître leurs droits; cette reconnaissance les aidera à préserver leur culture, leur identité, leurs coutumes, leurs traditions et leurs langues.

En vertu de l'article 25 de la Charte, on ne peut invoquer une autre disposition de cette Charte pour porter atteinte aux droits spéciaux des autochtones, droits qu'ils possèdent déjà ou qu'ils pourraient acquérir dans le futur. Par exemple, tout avantage qui serait accordé aux autochtones en vertu d'un règlement de revendications territoriales ne pourrait aller à l'encontre des droits à l'égalité énoncés dans la Charte.

L'article 35 de la *Loi constitutionnelle* confirme les droits existants, ancestraux ou issus de traités, des peuples autochtones du Canada.

La *Loi constitutionnelle* contient aussi un engagement écrit selon lequel, dans une période d'un an après l'entrée en vigueur de la *Loi constitutionnelle*, le premier ministre convoquera une conférence constitutionnelle dont l'ordre du jour devra comporter un point portant

Maintien des
autres droits
et libertés

26. Le fait que la présente charte garantit certains droits et libertés ne constitue pas une négation des autres droits ou libertés qui existent au Canada.

Maintien du
patrimoine
culturel

27. Toute interprétation de la présente charte doit concorder avec l'objectif de promouvoir le maintien et la valorisation du patrimoine multiculturel des Canadiens.

« *Dans ce nouveau Parlement, il n'y aura pas de questions de race, de nationalité, de religion ou de localité ... La raison d'agir des délégués à la conférence de Québec, en préparant les résolutions, a été de rendre justice à tous, justice à toutes les races, à toutes les religions, à toutes les nationalités et à tous les intérêts... »*

Sir Hector-Louis Langevin, Père de la Confédération, 1865.

sur la question des droits des peuples autochtones du Canada. Les représentants des autochtones seront invités à participer à cette conférence.

Cet article stipule qu'en accordant des garanties à certains droits et libertés dans la Charte, on ne nie pas l'existence d'autres droits. Autrement dit, la Charte ne prétend pas être un document complet traitant de tous les droits des Canadiens. Elle ne fait que reconnaître officiellement des droits *minimums*. Il n'y a rien dans la Charte qui empêchera le Parlement ou les assemblées législatives de prendre des mesures visant à accroître la protection de nos droits.

Les Canadiens peuvent être fiers du fait que ce pays ne soit pas devenu un creuset où les peuples qui l'ont formé ont perdu leur identité; au contraire, le Canada a pu conserver son caractère multiculturel. La réalité multiculturelle du pays est reconnue de façon officielle dans la Constitution au moyen des dispositions de la Charte stipulant que celle-ci doit être interprétée de façon à préserver et à mettre en valeur le patrimoine multiculturel du Canada.

« *Car ici (au Canada), je veux que le marbre reste le marbre; je veux que le granite reste le granite; je veux que le chêne reste le chêne; et de tous ces éléments, je veux faire une nation qui sera parmi les plus grandes du monde.* »

Sir Wilfrid Laurier, premier ministre du Canada, 1903.

« *Le Canada est un jardin ... dans lequel on a transplanté les fleurs les plus vivaces et les plus rayonnantes de nombreux autres pays, chacune conservant dans son nouvel environnement les meilleures des qualités pour lesquelles elle était aimée et prisée dans son pays natal...* »

Le très honorable John Diefenbaker, 1961.

Égalité de garantie des droits pour les deux sexes

28. Indépendamment des autres dispositions de la présente charte, les droits et libertés qui y sont mentionnés sont garantis également aux personnes des deux sexes.

Maintien des droits relatifs à certaines écoles

29. Les dispositions de la présente charte ne portent pas atteinte aux droits ou privilèges garantis en vertu de la Constitution du Canada concernant les écoles séparées et autres écoles confessionnelles.

Cette disposition spéciale confirme que tous les droits énoncés dans la Charte sont garantis tant aux hommes qu'aux femmes. Cette clause fut ajoutée à la demande des groupements féministes afin que la protection des droits des femmes soit bien assurée. Il s'agit d'une garantie qui ne *pourra pas* être annulée par une décision d'une assemblée législative ou du Parlement.

Aucune disposition de la Charte ne peut empêcher l'établissement et le fonctionnement d'écoles confessionnelles.

Grâce à cette clause par exemple, on ne peut pas invoquer la liberté de conscience, de religion ou les droits à l'égalité pour enfreindre les droits constitutionnels existants qui ont trait à la création et au finance-

Application aux
territoires

**30. Dans la présente charte, les dispositions qui visent
les provinces, leur législature ou leur assemblée
législative visent également le territoire du Yukon, les
territoires du Nord-Ouest ou leurs autorités législatives
compétentes.**

Non-élargissement
des compétences
législatives

**31. La présente charte n'élargit pas les compétences
législatives de quelque organisme ou autorité que ce
soit.**

ment par l'État d'écoles confessionnelles où les étudiants et les professeurs sont recrutés en fonction de leur appartenance à une croyance religieuse particulière.

Cet article précise que toutes les dispositions de la Charte s'appliquent au Yukon et aux Territoires du Nord-Ouest, de la même façon qu'aux provinces.

Cet article énonce de façon claire que rien dans la Charte n'a pour effet de modifier la répartition des pouvoirs du Parlement et des assemblées législatives découlant de l'*Acte de l'Amérique du Nord britannique*. La Charte ne retire aucun pouvoir aux provinces au profit du gouvernement fédéral non plus qu'elle n'en retire au fédéral au profit des provinces. La Charte ne fait que garantir aux Canadiens la jouissance de leurs droits fondamentaux sans restriction abusive de la part des deux ordres de gouvernement.

La Charte protège les droits et libertés des citoyens contre les actions des gouvernements. Ce sont les lois fédérales et provinciales traitant des droits de la personne qui continueront à assurer la protection des droits des individus entre eux.

Application de la charte

32. (1) La présente charte s'applique :
   a) au Parlement et au gouvernement du Canada, pour tous les domaines relevant du Parlement, y compris ceux qui concernent le territoire du Yukon et les territoires du Nord-Ouest;
   b) à la législature et au gouvernement de chaque province, pour tous les domaines relevant de cette législature.

(2) Par dérogation au paragraphe (1), l'article 15 n'a d'effet que trois ans après l'entrée en vigueur du présent article.

33. (1) Le Parlement ou la législature d'une province peut adopter une loi où il est expressément déclaré que celle-ci ou une de ses dispositions a effet indépendamment d'une disposition donnée de l'article 2 ou des articles 7 à 15 de la présente charte.

(2) La loi ou la disposition qui fait l'objet d'une déclaration conforme au présent article et en vigueur a l'effet qu'elle aurait sauf la disposition en cause de la charte.

(3) La déclaration visée au paragraphe (1) cesse d'avoir effet à la date qui y est précisée ou, au plus tard, cinq ans après son entrée en vigueur.

(4) Le Parlement ou une législature peut adopter de nouveau une déclaration visée au paragraphe (1).

(5) Le paragraphe (3) s'applique à toute déclaration adoptée sous le régime du paragraphe (4).

Sous réserve de l'exception suivante, dès son entrée en vigueur au moment du rapatriement, la Charte s'appliquera aux autorités gouvernementales fédérales, provinciales et territoriales. L'article 15, qui traite des droits à l'égalité, ne s'appliquera que trois ans plus tard.

Le délai de trois ans qui sera requis pour l'application des droits à l'égalité est nécessaire pour permettre au gouvernement fédéral, aux provinces et aux territoires de passer en revue et de modifier au besoin les lois qui ne seraient pas conformes aux garanties maintenant reconnues dans cet article. Ceci permettra d'éliminer un grand nombre de poursuites judiciaires coûteuses et superflues.

Selon les termes de l'accord qui a permis de sortir de l'impasse constitutionnelle, le Parlement et les législatures provinciales conserveront un pouvoir limité d'adopter des lois qui pourraient entrer en conflit avec les articles de la Charte traitant des libertés fondamentales, des garanties juridiques et des droits à l'égalité.

Pour pouvoir adopter de telles lois cependant, le Parlement ou la législature d'une province devra déclarer de façon expresse que la loi en question est adoptée *nonobstant* les dispositions spécifiques pertinentes de la Charte des droits.

En outre, toute clause « nonobstant » (ou dérogatoire) contenue dans une loi fédérale ou provinciale, devra être revue et adoptée à nouveau tous les cinq ans, sans quoi elle ne pourra demeurer en vigueur.

En bref, si un gouvernement devait proposer une loi dont l'effet serait de porter atteinte à certains des droits et libertés énoncés dans la Charte, ce gouvernement devrait déclarer clairement que c'est bien là ce qu'il entend faire et devrait ainsi accepter pleinement ses responsabilités et les conséquences politiques qui s'ensuivraient.

38

« ... (la clause nonobstant) pourrait de fait encourager les tribunaux à faire preuve de plus d'imagination que ce n'a été le cas jusqu'à présent. Ce fut l'une des craintes des gens qui étaient opposés à la Charte des droits : le dossier de l'interprétation judiciaire de la Charte existante n'a pas été très reluisant. Il est bien possible que le résultat des dispositions de la présente Charte quant à la protection des libertés civiles puisse être un jeu entre les tribunaux et le Parlement. Autrement dit, il vous sera impossible de porter atteinte aux droits de la personne sans rendre évident le fait que c'est bien ce que vous voulez faire; en même temps, les tribunaux vont pouvoir déclarer qu'une certaine loi entre en conflit avec la Charte. Cette procédure contribuera à porter le problème à l'attention du public. »

Le professeur Walter Tarnopolsky, ancien président de l'Association canadienne des libertés civiles, lors d'une interview accordée à **Sunday Morning**, à la radio de Radio-Canada, le 8 novembre 1981.

« Les clauses « nonobstant » constitueront un signal pour les partis d'opposition et pour la presse ... Politiquement, il sera très difficile pour un gouvernement de passer par-dessus la Charte. Cela constituera donc une protection suffisante pour la Charte. »

« Le système politique canadien est une démocratie parlementaire dans laquelle la volonté du Parlement est au-dessus de tout. S'il n'y avait pas de clause nonobstant dans la nouvelle Constitution, cette suprématie serait transférée aux tribunaux qui devraient décider si oui ou non une loi entre en conflit avec la Constitution. »

Il est important de noter ici qu'une clause « nonobstant » n'est pas du tout la même chose qu'une « clause de retrait ». Il est bien sûr qu'aucune province ne pourra choisir de ne pas être liée par la Charte des droits et libertés.

De plus, comme on l'a mentionné plus tôt, le pouvoir d'adopter des clauses « nonobstant » assure aux législatures, plutôt qu'aux tribunaux, le dernier mot sur les grandes questions de politique, de sorte que la Charte continuera d'être à l'image des valeurs de notre société en pleine évolution.

Il n'y a rien de nouveau dans le concept d'une clause « nonobstant ». Il existe déjà des clauses semblables dans l'*Alberta Bill of Rights,* dans le *Saskatchewan Human Rights Code,* dans la *Charte québécoise des droits et libertés de la personne* et dans la *Déclaration canadienne des droits.*

« Le fait de rendre légalement possible et à la fois politiquement difficile le fait de passer par-dessus la Charte constitue une sorte d'unification des deux notions ... Le résultat en est que la Charte est forte mais que tout de même, il existe une porte de sortie pour les législatures. »

Nouvelle de la Presse canadienne rapportant les propos de M⁴ Alan Borovoy, avocat-conseil de l'Association canadienne des libertés civiles, dans le journal The Calgary Herald, *le 7 novembre 1981.*

Titre

Titre

34. Titre de la présente partie : *Charte canadienne des droits et libertés.*

« L'adoption d'une charte des droits serait un acte public qui viendrait confirmer le rêve que nous nourrissons tous de vivre libres et égaux devant la loi, partout à travers le Canada. »

M. Claude Ryan, Cercle national des journalistes, Ottawa, le 12 décembre 1981.

. Cet article prévoit que la Charte sera connue sous le titre de *Charte canadienne des droits et libertés.*

Si vous désirez obtenir de plus amples renseignements au sujet de vos droits vous pouvez, dans un premier temps, communiquer avec votre député fédéral, votre député provincial ou avec l'un des organismes suivants.

Pour tout renseignement sur l'égalité des droits, prière de s'adresser à:

La Commission canadienne des droits de la personne

Bureau national:

Commission canadienne
  des droits de la personne
257, rue Slater
Ottawa (Ontario)
K1A 1E1

Région d'Ontario

Édifice Arthur Meighen
55, avenue St. Clair est
Pièce 623
Toronto (Ontario)
M4T 1M2

Région de l'Atlantique

Adresse du bureau:

Lord Nelson Arcade
Pièce 212
5675, chemin Spring Garden
Halifax (Nouvelle-Écosse)
B3J 1H1

Adresse postale:

C.P. 3545
Succursale Halifax-Sud
Halifax (Nouvelle-Écosse)
B3J 3J2

Région des Prairies

Édifice Kensington
275, avenue Portage
Pièce 1804
Winnipeg (Manitoba)
R3B 2B3

Région du Québec

2021, avenue Union
Pièce 1115
Montréal (Québec)
H3A 2S9

Région de l'Ouest

Édifice Montreal Trust
789, rue Pender ouest
Pièce 1002
Vancouver
(Colombie-Britannique)
V6C 1H2

Pour tout renseignement sur le droit des femmes, prière de s'adresser à:

Le Conseil consultatif canadien de la situation de la femme

66, rue Slater
18e étage
C.P. 1541, succursale B
Ottawa (Canada)
K1P 5R5

666, rue Sherbrooke ouest
Pièce 205
Montréal (Québec)
H3A 1E7

269, rue Main, pièce 600
Winnipeg (Manitoba)
R3C 1B2

C.P. 5174
Vancouver (Colombie-Britannique)
V6B 4B2

Pour tout renseignement sur les droits en matière de langues officielles, prière de s'adresser à:

Commissaire aux langues officielles

Bureau national

66, rue Slater
Ottawa (Canada)
K1A 0T8

170, rue Marian
Winnipeg (Manitoba)
R2H 0T4

Manitoba, Saskatchewan et le Nord-Ouest ontarien

C.P. 96
Norwood Grove
Winnipeg (Manitoba)
R2H 3B8

Alberta, Colombie-Britannique, Yukon et Territoires du Nord-Ouest

Édifice Liberty
10506, avenue Jasper
11e étage
Edmonton (Alberta)
T5J 2W9

Le centre et l'ouest de l'Ontario

127, rue Cedar
6e étage
Sudbury (Ontario)
P3E 1B1

Québec

615, boulevard Dorchester ouest
6e étage
Montréal (Québec)
H3B 1P5

Provinces de l'Atlantique

C.P. 1125
Moncton (Nouveau-Brunswick)
E1C 8P6

Pour tout renseignement sur les langues officielles dans la Fonction publique, notamment la mise à la disposition du public des services fédéraux dans les deux langues officielles et leur usage comme langue de travail, prière de s'adresser à:

Direction des langues
officielles
Secrétariat du Conseil du Trésor
Immeuble Vanier
222, rue Nepean
Ottawa (Canada)
K1A 0R5

Annexe A

Groupes et individus qui ont témoigné devant le Comité mixte spécial du Sénat et de la Chambre des communes sur la Constitution (par ordre alphabétique).

Aird, P. L., professeur, Faculté des forêts, Université de Toronto
Alliance pour la vie
Association canadienne des chefs de police
Association canadienne des commissaires d'écoles catholiques
Association canadienne des compagnies d'assurance-vie
Association canadienne des lesbiennes et des hommes gais
Association canadienne des libertés civiles
Association canadienne des procureurs de la Couronne
Association canadienne des travailleurs sociaux
Association canadienne du Barreau, Section de Terre-Neuve
Association canadienne française de l'Ontario
Association canadienne pour le droit à l'avortement
Association canadienne pour les déficients mentaux
Association culturelle franco-canadienne de la Saskatchewan
Association des droits de la personne de la Saskatchewan
Association des femmes autochtones du Canada
Association des Indiens de l'Alberta
Association des Iroquois et des Indiens alliés
Association des libertés civiles de la Colombie-Britannique
Association des Métis et des Indiens non inscrits de la Saskatchewan
Association du Barreau canadien
Association nationale de la femme et le droit
Association nationale des Canadiens d'origine japonaise
Bureau des écoles protestantes du Grand Montréal
«Business Council on National Issues»
Campagne Vie Canada
«Canada West Foundation»
«Canadian Committee on Learning Opportunities for Women»
«Canadians for Canada»
«Canadians for One Canada»
Centre pour la défense de l'intérêt public
Chambre de Commerce de l'Alberta
Chambre de Commerce du Canada
Chrétien, Jean, (L'honorable), ministre de la Justice et Procureur général du Canada
Club Media du Canada
Coalition des organisations provinciales pour les handicapés
Coalition pour la protection de la vie humaine
Comité d'action positive
Comité germano-canadien de la Constitution
Comité Inuit sur les affaires nationales
Comité mennonite central
Comité national d'action sur le statut de la femme
Comités de l'éducation confessionnelle de Terre-Neuve

Commission canadienne des droits de la personne
Commission des droits de l'homme du Nouveau-Brunswick
Conférence des évêques catholiques de l'Ontario
Conférence des évêques catholiques du Canada
Congrès juif canadien
Congrès national des Italo-Canadiens
Congrès polono-canadien
Conseil Algonquin
Conseil Attikamik-Montagnais
Conseil canadien de développement social
Conseil canadien de l'enfance et de la jeunesse
Conseil consultatif canadien de la situation de la femme
Conseil consultatif canadien du multiculturalisme
Conseil de la tribu Nishga
Conseil de la tribu Nuu-Chah-Nulth
Conseil des minorités du Québec
Conseil des organismes nationaux ethnoculturels du Canada
Conseil national des autochtones du Canada
«Council for Yukon Indians»
Église de Jésus-Christ des saints des derniers jours
Église unie du Canada
Fédération canadienne des associations des libertés civiles et
    des droits de l'homme
Fédération canadienne des municipalités
Fédération canadienne du civisme
Fédération des écoles indépendantes du Canada
Fédération des francophones hors Québec
Fédération des Indiens de la Saskatchewan
Fondation afro-asiatique du Canada
Fraternité nationale des Indiens
Gouvernement de la Nouvelle-Écosse
Gouvernement de la Saskatchewan
Gouvernement de l'Île-du-Prince-Édouard
Gouvernement des Territoires du Nord-Ouest
Gouvernement du Nouveau-Brunswick
Gouvernement du Territoire du Yukon
«Indian Rights for Indian Women»
Institut canadien national des aveugles
Liaison canadienne
Ligue nationale des Noirs du Canada
Love, Dean D. V.
Ministère de la Justice
Mouvement canadien pour une fédération mondiale
«National association of Japanese Canadians»
Nouveau Parti démocratique de l'Alberta
Organisation nationale d'anti-pauvreté
Parti Crédit social de l'Alberta
Parti de l'Union nationale du Québec
Parti progressiste conservateur de la Saskatchewan
«The People's Law School Society and Social Planning and Review
Council of British Columbia»
Russell, Peter H.

Société canadienne pour la prévention du crime
Société franco-manitobaine
«Ukrainian Canadian Committee»
Union des Indiens de la Nouvelle-Écosse
Union des Indiens de l'Ontario
Union des Indiens du Nouveau-Brunswick
«Vancouver Peoples' Law School Society»
Yalden, M. F., Commissaire aux langues officielles

Annexe B

Groupements et particuliers qui, en date du 2 février 1981, avaient fait une présentation au Comité mixte spécial du Sénat et de la Chambre des communes.

A

Abbass, Cyril J. – Willowdale, Ontario
Adams, Grethyll – Prince Albert, Saskatchewan
Adams, Helen – Collingwood, Ontario
Addington, Charles – London, Ontario
Adler, Simon – Kitchener, Ontario
«Affiliation of Multicultural Societies of British
  Columbia» – Kamloops, Colombie-Britannique
Agarwal, S. C. – Mississauga, Ontario
Agudath, Israël – Toronto, Ontario
Aird, Deborah – London, Ontario
Aird, Paul L. – Toronto, Ontario
Albert, J. M. – Vancouver, Colombie-Britannique
«Alberta Chamber of Commerce» – Edmonton, Alberta
«Alberta Committee of Action Groups of the Disabled» –
  Calgary, Alberta
«Alberta Lesbian and Gay Rights Association» – Edmonton,
  Alberta
«Alberta Liberal Party» – Calgary, Alberta
«Alberta New Democratic Party» – Edmonton, Alberta
«Alberta Public Policy Committee» – Edmonton, Alberta
«Alberta Real Estate Association» – Calgary, Alberta

«Alberta Status of Women Action Committee» – Edmonton,
   Alberta
«Alberta Women for Constitution Change» – Calgary, Alberta
Albo, Carol – Rossland, Colombie-Britannique
Alcock, Stuart – Vancouver, Colombie-Britannique
Aldwinckle, Mary C. – Ottawa, Ontario
«Algonquin Council» – Val d'Or, Québec
Allen, H. – Ouathiaski Cove, Colombie-Britannique
Alliance pour la vie – Winnipeg, Manitoba
Allier, Irène – Montréal, Québec
Allison, E. F. – Calgary, Alberta
Allistone, Ernie F. – Vancouver, Colombie-Britannique
Amdur, Reuel S. – Toronto, Ontario
Amys, John Hewitt – Toronto, Ontario
Anderson, Bruce W. – Frédéricton, Nouveau-Brunswick
Anderson Lake Band – D'Arcy, Colombie-Britannique
Andrews, Ralph – Edmonton, Alberta
«Anglican Church of Canada» – Toronto, Ontario
«Anglican Church of Canada» – London, Ontario
Angus, J. F. – Calgary, Alberta
Ardito, Ann
Ardito, Dorothy
Ardito, John E.
Ardito, Mary
Ardito, Paul J.
Ardito, Paul M.
Archer, R. Douglas – Vancouver, Colombie-Britannique
Armitage, D. P. – Brampton, Ontario
Armstrong, Ralph C. – Edmonton, Alberta
Assad, Jocelyne
Asselstine, Asta – Winnipeg, Manitoba
Association canadienne des commissaires des écoles
   catholiques – Toronto, Ontario
Association canadienne des chefs de police – Ottawa, Ontario
Association canadienne des compagnies d'assurance-vie –
   Toronto, Ontario
Association canadienne de l'immeuble – Don Mills (Toronto),
   Ontario
Association canadienne des écoles de service social – Ottawa,
   Ontario
Association canadienne des lesbiennes et des hommes
   gais – Ottawa, Ontario
Association canadienne des libertés civiles – Toronto, Ontario
Association canadienne des paraplégiques – Toronto, Ontario
Association canadienne des Procureurs de la Couronne –
   Toronto, Ontario
Association canadienne des travailleurs sociaux – Ottawa,
   Ontario
Association canadienne pour la santé mentale – Toronto,
   Ontario
Association canadienne pour le droit à l'avortement
   (ACDA) – Toronto, Ontario

Association canadienne pour les déficients mentaux – Toronto, Ontario

Association d'aide juridique de la communauté de Vancouver – Vancouver, Colombie-Britannique

Association des francophones du Nord-Ouest de l'Ontario – Thunder Bay, Ontario

Association des Indiens de l'Alberta – Edmonton, Alberta

Association des juristes d'expression française de l'Ontario – Ottawa, Ontario

Association des Métis et des Indiens non inscrits de la Saskatchewan – Regina, Saskatchewan

Association des parents catholiques (section anglaise) de la commission scolaire – Stormont, Dundas, Glengarry (Conseil des écoles séparées) – Ottawa, Ontario

Association du Barreau canadien – Ottawa, Ontario

Association du Barreau canadien (section Colombie-Britannique)

Association du Labrador québécois – Les Grondines, Québec

«Associated Disabled Persons of B.C.» – Victoria, Colombie-Britannique

Association canadienne-française de l'Ontario, Conseil régional des Mille-Îles – Kingston, Ontario

«Association of Canadian Clubs» – Ottawa, Ontario

Association canadienne d'éducation de langue française – Sillery, Québec

Association canadienne-française de l'Alberta – Edmonton, Alberta

ACFO – Windsor, Ontario

ACFO – Cornwall, Ontario

ACFO – Ottawa, Ontario

Association culturelle franco-canadienne de la Saskatchewan – Regina, Saskatchewan

Association forestière canadienne – Ottawa, Ontario

Association française des conseils scolaires de l'Ontario – Ottawa, Ontario

«Association of Gay Social Service Workers» – Toronto, Ontario

«Association of Iroquois and Allied Indians» – Wallaceburg, Ontario

Association nationale de la femme et le droit (A.N.F.D.) – Ottawa, Ontario

Assemblée nationale du Québec – Québec, Québec

Association pour le droit à la vie du N.-B. – Moncton, Nouveau-Brunswick

Association Progressiste conservatrice fédérale du Québec – Montréal, Québec

Athabaska Chipewyan Band 201 – Fort Chipewyan, Alberta

Atkinson College Council – Downsview, Ontario

Aultman, Richard – Powassan, Ontario

Aultman, Ruth – Powassan, Ontario

Austin, G. H. – Calgary, Alberta

Austman, Linda – Calgary, Alberta

Awan, Sadig Noor Alan – Ottawa, Ontario

B

Beachler, F. E. – Powassan, Ontario
Baer, Ted J. – Calgary, Alberta
Baig, B. Lee – Thunder Bay, Ontario
Bailey, Walter S. – Toronto, Ontario
Baker, Bryan J. N. – Don Mills, Ontario
Baker, Norman – Regina, Saskatchewan
The Baltic Federation in Canada – Toronto, Ontario
Bande de Beecher Bay – Nanaimo, Colombie-Britannique
Barabas, Joe – Guelph, Ontario
Barber-Starkey, Joe – Victoria, Colombie-Britannique
Barclay, Donald R. – Kitchener, Ontario
Barclay, Eric H. – Pickering, Ontario
Baril, Yves Réginald – Ottawa, Ontario
Barker, Harold W. – Scarborough, Ontario
Barman, Teresa – London, Ontario
Barrett, Bernice – Oshawa, Ontario
Barth, Joe – London, Ontario
Barrett, Erica – North Vancouver, Colombie-Britannique
Bartholomew, Michael – Ottawa, Ontario
Basavarajappa, K. G. – Nepean, Ontario
Basilian Fathers – Toronto, Ontario
Bawden, Edward – Montréal, Québec
Bearcroft, Norma – Salmon Arm, Colombie-Britannique
Beaton, Floyd M. – Powassan, Ontario
Beaton, John W. (M. et Mme) – Ajax, Ontario
Beaudry, Diane – St. Thomas, Ontario
Beaujot, Roderic – London, Ontario
Beauvais, Jean-Claude et Lisette – Hull, Québec
Beazley, Dorothy – Calgary, Alberta
Beckton, Clare F. – Halifax, Nouvelle-Écosse
Bédard, Daniel – Armstrong, Colombie-Britannique
Beecher, Leo P. – Toronto, Ontario
Beesley, Ken B. – Vancouver, Colombie-Britannique
Beeston, H. C. – Downsview, Ontario
Beeston, Marion – Downsview, Ontario
Beke, A. John – Regina, Saskatchewan
Béland, André – Beauport, Québec
Belfry, Rob – London, Ontario
Belkin, Elliott J. – Vancouver, Colombie-Britannique
Bell, Jim – Calgary, Alberta
Bell, Ronald G. – Peterborough, Ontario
Bennett, Ferne – Toronto, Ontario
Benson, Quennie et Robert – Toronto, Ontario
Benton, S. B. – Frédéricton, Nouveau-Brunswick
Bentz, Peter – Thunder Bay, Ontario
Berdan, Jack – Alvinston, Ontario
Berg, John H. – Calgary, Alberta
Berge, Anne et Lawrence – Pickering, Ontario
Bernard, H. H. – London, Ontario

Bernarz, John – Iroquois Falls, Ontario
Bertrand, Daniel – Dorval, Québec
«Bible Holiness Movement» – Vancouver, Colombie-
Britannique
Bickis, Mikelis G. – Ottawa, Ontario
Biggs, Evelyn V. – White Rock, Colombie-Britannique
Birch, G. S. – Calgary, Alberta
Bird, William E. – Belleville, Ontario
Black, William – Vancouver, Colombie-Britannique
Blakely, H. C. – Regina, Saskatchewan
«Blind Organization of Ontario with Selfhelp Tactics» –
Toronto, Ontario
Blitstein, G. – Aldergrove, Colombie-Britannique
«Blueberry Band» – Blueberry Reserve, Colombie-Britannique
«Board of Education for the City of Toronto» – Toronto,
Ontario
Bob, Wannita – Vedder Crossing, Manitoba
Bockmann, Walter – Toronto, Ontario
Boehm, Arnold H. – Ottawa, Ontario
Boehnke, Richard – Islington, Ontario
Boivin, Pierre – Québec, Québec
Bolwerk, Peter – Powassan, Ontario
Bordeleau, André G. – Guelph, Ontario
Borough of Etobicoke – Etobicoke, Ontario
Boucher, Ken – Mission, Colombie-Britannique
Boucher, Lillian – Ottawa, Ontario
Boucquez, Doug – Cobourg, Ontario
Bourget, Clément – Montréal, Québec
Bouri, Mary
Bouri, Terry
Bowyer, Joseph – Windsor, Ontario
Boyle, Merrijane – St. Paul, Nouveau-Brunswick
Boyle, Theresa M. – Mississauga, Ontario
Bradford, Art – Orillia, Ontario
Braunberger, H. A. – Orléans, Ontario
Brennan, J. – Islington, Ontario
Brewis, D. W. – Victoria, Colombie-Britannique
Briggs, Robert S. B. B. – Surrey, Colombie-Britannique
Brisbin, J. E. – Three Hills, Alberta
«British Columbia Chamber of Commerce» – Vancouver,
Colombie-Britannique
«British Columbia Civil Liberties Association» – Vancouver,
Colombie-Britannique
«British Columbia Human Rights Symposium» – Vernon,
Colombie-Britannique
«British Columbia Medical Association» – Vancouver,
Colombie-Britannique
«British Columbia Provincial Council of Carpenters» –
Vancouver, Colombie-Britannique
Britton, Sid H. – Aurora, Ontario
Brock, Georgia – Port Perry, Ontario
Brooks, Kathleen – London, Ontario

Brooks, Lorne – Calgary, Alberta
Brooks, Phillip – Fort Saskatchewan, Alberta
Brooymans, Mary Ann – Port Stanley, Ontario
Brow, Betty – Vancouver, Colombie-Britannique
Brown, Anne J. – Calgary, Alberta
Brown, Helen R. – Saskatoon, Saskatchewan
Browne, G. P. – Ottawa, Ontario
Brunelle, Jacques M. – Sudbury, Ontario
Bruning, O. H. – Swift Current, Saskatchewan
Brunton, Richard – Ottawa, Ontario
Brunton, William – Simcoe, Ontario
Bryson, Peter M. – Halifax, Nouvelle-Écosse
Bubar, S. L. – Midway, Colombie-Britannique
Buck, Frank – Lantzville, Colombie-Britannique
Buck, Zena – Lantzville, Colombie-Britannique
Bufton, Audrey – Ottawa, Ontario
Bureau des écoles protestantes du Grand-Montréal –
    Montréal, Québec
Burness, James N. – Lethbridge, Alberta
«Burrard Indian Band» – Vancouver Nord, Colombie-
    Britannique
Busby, William C. – Scarborough, Ontario
«Business Council on National Issues» – Toronto, Ontario
Bustard, Ernest E. – Oakville, Ontario
Butler, David E. – Calgary, Alberta
Buttery, J. W. L. – Galiano, Colombie-Britannique
Bydwell, Howard William – Kingston, Ontario

C

Cain, Sandy – Niagara Falls, Ontario
Caldwell, M. C. – Calgary, Alberta
«Calgary Action Group of the Disabled» – Calgary, Alberta
«Calgary Civil Liberties Association» – Calgary, Alberta
Camateros, Stylianos – Sainte-Foy, Québec
Cameron, Don – Kamloops, Colombie-Britannique
Cameron, Neil – Minnedosa, Manitoba
Cameron, Norma – Ottawa, Ontario
Campagne Vie Canada – Edmonton, Alberta
Campbell, A. J. – Nepean, Ontario
Campbell, Dorothy J. – Halifax, Nouvelle-Écosse
Campbell, Jean D. – Toronto, Ontario
Campbell, Margaret – Vernon, Colombie-Britannique
Campbell, Maurice R. – Vancouver, Colombie-Britannique
Campbell, R. – Vernon, Colombie-Britannique
«Camrose R. C. Separate School District No. 60» – Camrose,
    Alberta
«Canadian Bureau of the North American Jewish Students'
    Network» – Toronto, Ontario
«Canadian Cattle Consultants» – Calgary, Alberta
«Canadian Citizens Constitution Committee» – Calgary,
    Alberta
«Canadian Committee for the International Union for Conser-

vation of Nature and Natural Resources» – Ottawa, Ontario

«Canadian Committee on Learning Opportunities for Women» – Toronto, Ontario

«Canadian Association for the Mentally Retarded» – Downsview (Toronto), Ontario

«Canadian Congress for Learning Opportunities for Women» – Toronto, Ontario

«Canadian Copyright Institute» – Toronto, Ontario

«Canadian Health Coalition» – Ottawa, Ontario

«Canadian Indian Lawyers' Association» – Regina, Saskatchewan

«Canadian League of Rights» – Flesherton, Ontario

«Canadian Organization of Small Business» – Edmonton, Alberta

«Canadian Parents for French» – Ottawa, Ontario

«Canadian Parents for French, Alberta Branch» – Calgary, Alberta

«Canadian Physicians for Life» – Hamilton, Ontario

«Canadian Slovak League» – Ottawa, Ontario

«Canadian Society for Professional Engineers» – Toronto, Ontario

«Canadian Sebobran» – Hamilton, Ontario

«Canadians for Canada» – Grafton, Ontario

«Canadians in Defence of Labour Rights» – Toronto, Ontario

«Canadians for One Canada» – Winnipeg, Manitoba

«Canadians for Responsible Government» – Ottawa, Ontario

«Canadians United for Separation of Church and State» – Vancouver, Colombie-Britannique

«Cape Breton Right to Life» – Sydney, Nouvelle-Écosse

Carbonneau, Louis-Roy – Québec, Québec

«Cardinal Léger Secondary School» – Brampton, Ontario

Carmichael, Dolina A. – Edmonton, Alberta

Carrier, Jean – Thetford Mines, Québec

Carroll, Joseph P. – Ajax, Ontario

Carruthers, Allan – Vancouver, Colombie-Britannique

Carruthers, Joanne – Cambridge, Ontario

Carson, William – Vancouver, Colombie-Britannique

Carson, Kathleen – Vancouver, Colombie-Britannique

Carson, Andrew R. – Vancouver, Colombie-Britannique

Caswell, Gay White – Saskatoon, Saskatchewan

«Catholic Women's League of Canada» – Winnipeg, Manitoba

«Catholic Women's League of Canada, Sault Sainte-Marie Regional Council» – Sault Sainte-Marie, Ontario

Celentano, Shirley – North Bay, Ontario

«Centre for Continuing Education» –Halifax, Nouvelle-Écosse

Le Centre pour la défense de l'intérêt public – Ottawa, Ontario

Chahley, William – Rothesay, Nouveau-Brunswick

La Chambre de Commerce de Calgary – Calgary, Alberta

La Chambre de Commerce du Canada – Montréal, Québec

Chataway, Peter J. – Kelowna, Colombie-Britannique

«Cheslatta Band» – Cheslatta Indian Reserve, Colombie-Britannique

Cheston, Bruce et Linda – Regina, Saskatchewan

Chevaliers de Colomb, Conseil nº 6881 – Clarence Creek, Ontario

Childs, Fred et famille – Calgary, Alberta

Chillingworth, N. Lorraine – Nepean, Ontario

«Chinese Benevolent Association of Vancouver» – Vancouver, Colombie-Britannique

«Chinese-Canadian Council for Equality» – Vancouver, Colombie-Britannique

Chipmen, H. R. – Halifax, Nouvelle-Écosse

Chippendale, Anne – Calgary, Alberta

«Christian Labour Association of Canada» – Rexdale (Toronto), Ontario

«Christian Reformed Church of Williamsburg» – Williamsburg, Ontario

«Christian Science Committee on Publication for Ontario» – Toronto, Ontario

«Christian Science Federal Representative for Canada» – Toronto, Ontario

Christian, William – Guelph, Ontario

Church, Betty – Brampton, Ontario

«Citizens Association to Save the Environment» – Victoria, Colombie-Britannique

«The Citizens for More Time Committee» – Vernon, Colombie-Britannique

Clancy, Dorothy C. – Edmonton, Alberta

Clark, Keiron – Toronto, Ontario

Clark, Lynda-Anne – Ottawa, Ontario

Clarke, Alan – Ottawa, Ontario

Clarke, Anne – Victoria, Colombie-Britannique

Cleveland, George – McGrath, Alberta

Cloutier, Denys – Sherbrooke, Québec

Cloutier, Édouard – Montréal, Québec

Club Media du Canada – Saint-Jean, Nouveau-Brunswick

«Coalition for the Protection of Human Life» – Toronto, Ontario

Coalition des organismes provinciaux pour les handicapés – Winnipeg, Manitoba

Coats, David – Ajax, Ontario

Coates, H. (M. et Mme) – Prince George, Colombie-Britannique

Codling, Doug (pasteur) – Richmond, Colombie-Britannique

Cohen, Maxwell – Ottawa, Ontario

«Coldstream Friends Meeting» – Ilderton, Ontario

«Coldwater Indian Reserve» – Merritt, Colombie-Britannique

Coley, V. H. – Edmonton, Alberta

Coll, Philip – Guelph, Ontario

Collie, Ronald A. – Calgary, Alberta

Collins, John E. – Calgary, Alberta

Collyer, Muriel – Leamington, Ontario

Colwill-Maddock, M. – Muskoka Lake, Ontario

Comité consultatif de langue française, comté de Simcoe – Penetanguishene, Ontario

Le Comité culturel d'Oshawa – Oshawa, Ontario

Comité de l'éducation confessionnelle de Terre-Neuve – Saint-Jean, Terre-Neuve

Comité germano-canadien de la constitution – Ottawa, Ontario

Le Comité Inuit sur les affaires nationales – Ottawa, Ontario

Le Comité national d'action sur le statut de la femme – Toronto, Ontario

Comité ontarien sur la condition féminine – Toronto, Ontario

Comité national pour l'égalité linguistique (C.N.E.L.) – Montréal, Québec

Le Comité québécois pour les régions linguistiques – Montréal, Québec

Comité des communistes canadiens, section Vancouver – Vancouver, Colombie-Britannique

Commissaire aux langues officielles – Ottawa, Ontario

Commission canadienne des droits de la personne – Ottawa, Ontario

«Commission on Legislation and Civic Action of Agudath Israel of Canada» – Toronto, Ontario

«Committee of the Council of Disabled (National Capital Region)» – Ottawa, Ontario

«Committee of Canadian Communists» – Regina, Saskatchewan

«Committee for Constitutional Awareness» – Mississauga, Ontario

«Committee to Democratize the Constitutional Debate» – Toronto, Ontario

«Committee for Justice and Liberty Foundation» – Toronto, Ontario

«Committee for Racial Equality» – Toronto, Ontario

«Committee for Racial Justice» – Vancouver, Colombie-Britannique

«Community Business and Professional Association» – Vancouver, Colombie-Britannique

«Concerned Citizens of Toronto» – Toronto, Ontario

Conférence canadienne des Arts – Ottawa, Ontario

Conférence canadienne sur la religion et la paix mondiale – Toronto, Ontario

Conférence des évêques catholiques de l'Ontario – Toronto, Ontario

Conférence des évêques catholiques du Canada – Ottawa, Ontario

Congrès juif canadien – Montréal, Québec

Congrès des linguistes – Winnipeg, Manitoba

Congrès national des Italo-Canadiens, région du Québec – Montréal, Québec

Congrès polono-canadien – Toronto, Ontario

Congrès du travail du Canada – Ottawa, Ontario

Conklin, W. E. – Windsor, Ontario

Connely, Michael – Toronto, Ontario

Conroy, John W. – Mission, Colombie-Britannique

Conseil Attikamik-Montagnais – Ville des Hurons, Québec

Conseil canadien d'artisanat – Ottawa, Ontario

Conseil canadien de coordination de la déficience auditive – Ottawa, Ontario

Conseil canadien de l'enfance et de la jeunesse – Ottawa, Ontario

Conseil canadien des aveugles – London, Ontario

Conseil canadien de développement social – Ottawa, Ontario

Conseil canadien des Chrétiens et des Juifs – Vancouver, Colombie-Britannique

Conseil canadien pour la réadaptation des handicapés – Toronto, Ontario

Conseil canadien pour l'enfance exceptionnelle (Chapitre n° 475) – Québec

Conseil canadien pour les enfants exceptionnels – Vancouver, Colombie-Britannique

Conseil consultatif canadien de la situation de la femme – Ottawa, Ontario

Conseil consultatif canadien du multiculturalisme – Edmonton, Alberta

Conseil consultatif des citoyens de l'Ouest de l'Île de Montréal – Montréal, Québec

Conseil des écoles catholiques de Prescott-Russell – L'Orignal, Ontario

Conseil francophone de planification scolaire d'Ottawa-Carleton – Ottawa, Ontario

Conseil de la langue française du Québec – Québec, Québec

Conseil de la tribu Nishga – New Aiyansh, Colombie-Britannique

Conseil de la tribu Nuu-Chah-Nulth – Île de Vancouver, Colombie-Britannique

Conseil de vie française – Cornwall, Ontario

Conseil des Indiens du Yukon – Whitehorse, Yukon

Conseil des minorités du Québec – Montréal, Québec

Conseil des organismes nationaux ethnoculturels du Canada – Toronto, Ontario

Conseil du patronat de la Colombie-Britannique – Vancouver, Colombie-Britannique

Conseil du patronat du Québec – Montréal, Québec

Le Conseil économique des provinces de l'Atlantique – Halifax, Nouvelle-Écosse

Le Conseil national des autochtones du Canada – Ottawa, Ontario

Conseil national des femmes du Canada – Ottawa, Ontario

Conseil national des femmes juives du Canada – Downsview, Ontario

Conseil pour l'unité canadienne – Montréal, Québec

Conseil scolaire d'Ottawa – Ottawa, Ontario

«Conservation Council of Ontario» – Toronto, Ontario
Cook, Ernest – Powassan, Ontario
Cook, Lillian – Powassan, Ontario
Conway, Terry J. – Windsor, Ontario
Cooke, Ellen – Winnipeg, Manitoba
Cooper, K. Eilleen – Calgary, Alberta
Corcoran, Catherine – Islington, Ontario
Corcoran, Don – Islington, Ontario
Corcoran, Marg – Islington, Ontario
Corcoran, Pat – Islington, Ontario
Costly, Anne et famille – Burnaby, Colombie-Britannique
Côté, René – Laval, Québec
Coulter, L. A.
«Council of Christian Reformed Churches in Canada» –
   Burlington, Ontario
«Council of India Societies of Edmonton» – Edmonton, Alberta
«Council of Muslim Communities of Canada» – Ottawa,
   Ontario
«Council of the Quatsino Band – Quatsino Subdivision
   n° 18» – Colombie-Britannique
«Council of the Skookumchuck Band» – Mission, Colombie-
   Britannique
Cousins, Fred T. – Calgary, Alberta
Coutts, Thelma – Powassan, Ontario
Covey, W. – Chilliwack, Colombie-Britannique
«Cowichan Band Council» – Duncan, Colombie-Britannique
Coxon, Laura – Milverton, Ontario
Crawford-Craft, Hazel – Toronto, Ontario
Creed, George E. – Stoney Creek, Ontario
Creighton, Mary Martha – Tantallon, Nouvelle-Écosse
Crow, Stanley – Don Mills, Ontario
Crowe, Dolores – Saskatoon, Saskatchewan
Curran, Thomas H. – Halifax, Nouvelle-Écosse
Currie, D. V. – Edmonton, Alberta
Currier, N. – Nanaimo, Colombie-Britannique
«Czechoslovak Ethnic Community» – Edmonton, Alberta

D
Daigle, Kathleen B. – Whitby, Ontario
Daigle, Yvon – Sherbrooke, Québec
Dalcourt, Madeleine – Fenwick, Ontario
Danskin, Ruby – Burnaby, Colombie-Britannique
Darrach, Ian G. – Halifax, Nouvelle-Écosse
Davis, Jack – Victoria, Colombie-Britannique
Dawe, Douglas – Ottawa, Ontario
Dawe, H. W. – Ottawa, Ontario
Day, Jean – Sarnia, Ontario
Dean, Lewis – Halifax, Nouvelle-Écosse
Degoey, Josephine – Leamington, Ontario
Dekler, David – Ottawa, Ontario
Dejesus, John M. – Vancouver-Nord, Colombie-Britannique
de Lasala, Jennifer – Ottawa, Ontario

de Net, Va – Delhi
den Ouden, Marco – Coquitlam, Colombie-Britannique
Diebe, W. – Heffley Creek, Colombie-Britannique
Dignity Canada Dignité – Winnipeg, Manitoba
Dignity Edmonton Dignité – Edmonton, Alberta
Dignity Ottawa Dignité – Ottawa, Ontario
Dinnide, Howard – Weston, Ontario
Dinniwell, Donna – London, Ontario
Dion, Léon – Québec, Québec
Dionne, Albert – Sainte-Foy, Québec
Dionne, François – Cap-Rouge, Québec
Direction jeunesse – Ottawa, Ontario
Divertissements Emprise Inc. – Montréal, Québec
Doherty, M. M. – Penetanguishene, Ontario
«Doig River Band Fort Saint Jean & Prince George
  District» – Doig River Reserve, Colombie-Britannique
«The Dominion of Canada English-Speaking Association» –
  Dorchester, Nouveau-Brunswick
«Dominion of Canada Party» – Calgary, Alberta
Donald, G. Cameron – Edmonton, Alberta
Doswell, James W. – Oshawa, Ontario
Doull, J. A. – Halifax, Nouvelle-Écosse
Dove, Elizabeth – Kingston, Ontario
Drewer, J. – Edmonton, Alberta
Driedger, Elmer A. – Ottawa, Ontario
Duda, Michael – Halifax, Nouvelle-Écosse
Duffy, Rena – Willowdale, Ontario
Duguid, Alan T. – Calgary, Alberta
Dumontet, Elizabeth – Saskatoon, Saskatchewan
«Dunbarton-Fairport United Church» – Pickering, Ontario
Duncan, MacDonald W. – London, Ontario
Dunne, Patrick B. – Saint-Jean, Terre-Neuve
Duriez, Donald G. – Whitehorse, Yukon
Dyck, John E. – Halifax, Nouvelle-Écosse

E

Eastman Wynne – Waterloo, Ontario
Eayrs, Jonathan – Halifax, Nouvelle-Écosse
Edmonds, Hilda L. – Edmonton, Alberta
Edwards, David R. – Consort, Alberta
«Egerton Baptist Church» – London, Ontario
Église de Jésus-Christ des saints des derniers jours – Toronto,
  Ontario
L'Église unie du Canada – Edmonton, Alberta
Église La mission chrétienne évangélique – Sainte-Julie-de-
  Verchères, Québec
Eley, L. S. – Regina, Saskatchewan
Ellis, G. L. T. – Stevensville, Ontario
Ellis, John – Hamilton, Ontario
Emberley, Kenneth – Winnipeg, Manitoba
«Emergency Committee for the Defence of Religious
  Rights» – Guelph, Ontario

«Empire Loyalists Association (Governor Simcoe Branch)» –
Toronto, Ontario

English, F. W. – Trail, Colombie-Britannique

Enright, E. Marie – Saskatoon, Saskatchewan

Ermacora, Marco – Montréal, Québec

Esmonde-White, Robin – Charlottetown, Île-du-Prince-
Édouard

Etienne, Cindy – Cache Creek, Colombie-Britannique

Etienne, Gerald – Cache Creek, Colombie-Britannique

Euverman, Anne – Salmon Arm, Colombie-Britannique

Evans, Bernard – Yarker, Ontario

Evans, Helga – Coquitlam, Colombie-Britannique

Evans, Lucylle E. – Vancouver, Colombie-Britannique

Evans, W. D. – Calgary, Alberta

L'Express de la constitution – Ottawa, Ontario

F

Falconer, H. M. – Toronto, Ontario

Falconer, Janet – Chase, Colombie-Britannique

«The Family Life Bureau» – Saint-Jean, Terre-Neuve

«The Fane of the Psilocybe Mushroom» – Victoria,
Colombie-Britannique

Farrell, James H. – Toronto, Ontario

Faucher, Jean-Charles – Outremont, Québec

Fearn, Gordon, F. N. – Edmonton, Alberta

«Federated Anti-Poverty Group of B. C.» – Abbotsford,
Colombie-Britannique

«Federated Women's Institutes of Canada» – Ottawa, Ontario

La Fédération des associations de parents et d'instituteurs de
langue française d'Ontario – Ottawa, Ontario

La Fédération canadienne des associations des libertés civiles
et des droits de l'homme – Ottawa, Ontario

La Fédération canadienne du civisme – Ottawa, Ontario

La Fédération canadienne des clubs de femmes de carrières
libérales et commerciales – Ottawa, Ontario

Fédération canadienne des enseignants – Ottawa, Ontario

Fédération canadienne des femmes diplômées des universités –
Toronto, Ontario

Fédération canadienne des municipalités – Ottawa, Ontario

La Fédération des femmes canadiennes-françaises – Oshawa,
Ontario

La Fédération des francophones hors Québec – Ottawa,
Ontario

«Federation of Catholic Parent-Teacher Associations of
Ontario» – Ottawa, Ontario

«The Federation of Chinese Canadian Professionals
(Ontario)» – Toronto, Ontario

Fédération des écoles indépendantes du Canada – Vancouver,
Colombie-Britannique

Fédération des Indiens de la Saskatchewan – Prince Albert,
Saskatchewan

La Fédération nationale des retraités et citoyens âgés –
Toronto, Ontario

La Fédération pour le planning des naissances du Canada – Ottawa, Ontario

Fédération du travail de la Colombie-Britannique – Burnaby, Colombie-Britannique

Felhaleer, Carl (Mme) – Leamington, Ontario

Felsen, Marjorie – Victoria, Colombie-Britannique

Ferguson, Hugh J. – Chesley, Ontario

Fernandes, B. L. – Scarborough, Ontario

Ferrazzi, Giuseppe – Cambridge, Ontario

Fields, Harvey J. (Rabbi) – Toronto, Ontario

Filips, J. E. – Vancouver, Colombie-Britannique

Filliter, David F. – Saint-Jean, Nouveau-Brunswick

Finlayson, R. – Scarborough, Ontario

«Finnish-Canadian Cultural Federation» – Toronto, Ontario

Fish, J. R. – Calgary, Alberta

Fisher, Gabriella Du Vernet – Toronto, Ontario

Fitzmaurice, Peter J. – Bracebridge, Ontario

Fleming, M. L. – Midnapau, Alberta

Flis, Jesse P. – Ottawa, Ontario

La Fondation afro-asiatique du Canada – Montréal, Québec

Fondation canadienne des droits de l'homme – Montréal, Québec

La Fondation de l'Ouest canadien – Calgary, Alberta

Ford, Austin H. – Calgary, Alberta

Ford, Barbara A. – Calgary, Alberta

Ford, Dorothy – Brooks, Alberta

Forest, Georges – Saint-Boniface, Manitoba

Forsey, Eugene A. – Ottawa, Ontario

Forsyth, Margaret – Wolfville, Nouvelle-Écosse

Fortier, Jacques – Sainte-Foy, Québec

Fowler, Wendy P. – Oakville, Ontario

Fox, Jean G. – Calgary, Alberta

Fraser, Carol M. – Calgary, Alberta

Fraser, John A. (L'hon.) – Ottawa, Ontario

«Fraser Lake Band» – Fort Fraser, Colombie-Britannique

Fraser, Lewis (M. et Mme) – Mississauga, Ontario

Fraser, Neil A. – Sydenham, Ontario

Fraternité nationale des Indiens – Ottawa, Ontario

«Freedom of Choice Movement» – Montréal, Québec

«Freedom of Choice Party» – Montréal, Québec

Freeman, R. F. – Ottawa, Ontario

«French Association of Ontario School Boards» – Ottawa, Ontario

Frères du Sacré-Cœur – Ottawa, Ontario

Frey, John – Edmonton, Alberta

Frieser, Ann – Steinbach, Manitoba

Fulcher, James S. – Ottawa, Ontario

Furlong, T. E. – Saint-Jean, Terre-Neuve

G

Gaasenbeck, Karen B. – London, Ontario

Gambit Games – Chatham, Ontario

Garahan, Jim et Kathie – New Liskeard, Ontario
Gardner, J. Y. – Peackland, Colombie-Britannique
Garland, J. M. Boyd – Regina, Saskatchewan
Garrison, Philip – Montréal, Québec
Gaspire, Cyril et Marina – St. Thomas, Ontario
«Gay Fathers of Toronto» – Toronto, Ontario
Gentry, Peter – Petawawa, Ontario
Geraets, Théodore F. – Ottawa, Ontario
«The German Canadian Club of Red Deer» – Red Deer,
    Alberta
Gibson, Alan J. – Calgary, Alberta
Gibson, Everett – Powassan, Ontario
Gibson, Gertrude – Powassan, Ontario
Gierutto, Helena – Toronto, Ontario
Gilbert, Marc – Montréal, Québec
Gillate, Sidney F. – Penticton, Colombie-Britannique
Gilley, Donald R. – Calgary, Alberta
«Gitanmaax Band Council» – Hazelton, Colombie-Britannique
«Gitksan-Carrier Tribal Council» – Hazelton, Colombie-
    Britannique
Glass, J. G. – Calgary, Alberta
Goddard, Ruth – Cambridge, Ontario
Goddard, Teresa – Cambridge, Ontario
Godwin, G. – Calgary, Alberta
Good, I. – Cambridge, Ontario
Gordon, Bill – Calgary, Alberta
Gordon, Frances – Calgary, Alberta
Gorman, Ruth – Calgary, Alberta
Gorman, Ruth (Dr) – Calgary, Alberta
Goulden, L. N. – Edmonton, Alberta
Gouvernement de l'Alberta – Edmonton, Alberta
Gouvernement de la Colombie-Britannique – Victoria,
    Colombie-Britannique
Gouvernement du Nouveau-Brunswick – Frédéricton,
    Nouveau-Brunswick
Gouvernement de la Nouvelle-Écosse – Halifax, Nouvelle-
    Écosse
Gouvernement du Manitoba – Winnipeg, Manitoba
Gouvernement de l'Île-du-Prince-Édouard – Charlottetown,
    Île-du-Prince-Édouard
Gouvernement du Québec – Québec, Québec
Gouvernement de la Saskatchewan – Regina, Saskatchewan
Gouvernement des Territoires du Nord-Ouest – Yellowknife,
    Territoires du Nord-Ouest
Gouvernement du Yukon – Whitehorse, Yukon
Gralnoski, Joseph A. – Powassan, Ontario
«Grand Council Treaty No. 3» – Kenora, Ontario
«Grand Council Treaty No. 9» – Timmins, Ontario
«Grand Orange Lodge of Canada» – Frédéricton, Nouveau-
    Brunswick
Grant, Hugh – Toronto, Ontario
Graves, Joseph – Hamilton, Ontario

Grayson, Thomas B. – Scarborough, Ontario
Green, Sidney – Winnipeg, Manitoba
Greene, Ian – Parson, Colombie-Britannique
Greenfield, Robert S. – Metcalfe, Ontario
Greenwood, F. Murray – Vancouver, Colombie-Britannique
Griffiths, Ruth – Prince-Albert, Saskatchewan
Grolle, E. Hendrik – Regina, Saskatchewan
«Group for Survival» – Saskatoon, Saskatchewan
Grygier, Tadeusz – Ottawa, Ontario
Guttne, Nancy – Calgary, Alberta

H

Haddock, Yoland – Fernie, Colombie-Britannique
«Hagwilget Band Council» – New Hazelton, Colombie-
  Britannique
Hall, Fred – Longbow Lake Post Office, Ontario
Hall, Terry – Ottawa, Ontario
Hamilton, Ernest – Forthill, Ontario
Hamilton, Elinor – Forthill, Ontario
Hamilton, Gordon – Kelowna, Colombie-Britannique
Hamilton, W. D. – Frédéricton, Nouveau-Brunswick
Hammond, Jessie L. – West Vancouver, Colombie-
  Britannique
Hann, Ray – Winnipeg, Manitoba
Hansen, Albert – Wasaga Beach, Ontario
Hanson, Brian – Calgary, Alberta
Harder, Agatha – Ottawa, Ontario
Harder, Cornelius – Ottawa, Ontario
Hardy, Helen – Toronto, Ontario
Harris, William – London, Ontario
Hart, S. W. D. – Picton, Ontario
Hart, W. J. – Willowdale, Ontario
Harvie, André – Calgary, Alberta
Hatfield, H. R. – Penticton, Colombie-Britannique
Hauck, Margaret – Kitchener, Ontario
Hawkesworth, Bob – Calgary, Alberta
Haworth, D. – Aurora, Ontario
Hay, Joan A. – Port Alberni, Colombie-Britannique
Hay, W. – Winnipeg, Manitoba
Hayward, R. B. – Halifax, Nouvelle-Écosse
Heeney, Dennis H. – Brandon, Manitoba
Henderson, Anna – Toronto, Ontario
Henderson, Luci – Duntroon, Ontario
Hennessy, Peter H. – Elginburg, Ontario
Henry, Penny – Vedder Crossing, Colombie-Britannique
Herring, Joyce – Calgary, Alberta
Higgins, Catherine L.'– Islington, Ontario
Higgins, Catherine M. – Islington, Ontario
Higgins, Jerome – Islington, Ontario
Higgins, John A. – Islington, Ontario
Higgins, John P. – Islington, Ontario
Higgins, Mary Jane – Islington, Ontario

Hill, James Thomas – Sudbury, Ontario
Hillyer, Fred – Cardston, Alberta
Hind, M. – Calgary, Alberta
Hind, Peter – Calgary, Alberta
Hodgins, Barbara L. – Calgary, Alberta
Hodgson, W. George – Lindsay, Ontario
Hogan, William (Mme) – Powassan, Ontario
Hogg, Peter W. – Downsview, Ontario
Hogg, R. – Kelowna, Colombie-Britannique
Hollinger, Benjamin – Pembroke, Ontario
Holmes, Mildred V. – Sutton West, Ontario
Holy, Mary – Pickering, Ontario
Hooten, J. A. – Calgary, Alberta
Hooten, Maureen – Calgary, Alberta
Hooten, N. R. – Calgary, Alberta
Horton, Harry – Windsor, Ontario
Hough, Barbara J. – Halifax, Nouvelle-Écosse
Houle, Patricia – Sarnia, Ontario
Howard, Susan A. – Sarnia, Ontario
Howard, T. P. – Calgary, Alberta
Howden, Peter H. – Barrie, Ontario
Howe, Glen – Toronto, Ontario
Hubka, Brian F. – Coleman, Alberta
Hubscher, Frank Fred – Toronto, Ontario
Hughes, Ken – Edmonton, Alberta
«Human Action to Limit Taxes (HALT)» – Vancouver, Colombie-Britannique
«Human Rights Institute of Canada» – Ottawa, Ontario
Hummel, Dorothy – Powassan, Ontario
Hummel, Joe – Powassan, Ontario
Humphries, A. J. – Vancouver, Colombie-Britannique
Hunt, Glenda – Red Deer, Alberta
Hunt, G. Patrick – Mount Uniacke, Nouvelle-Écosse
Hunter, Allan D. – Calgary, Alberta
Husby, Philip J. – Winnipeg, Manitoba
Hutchings, Gertrude – High River, Alberta
Hypher, R. P. – Carrying Place, Ontario

I
Ibbitson, Clayton – Powassan, Ontario
Ibbitson, Jean – Powassan, Ontario
Iervella, Silvana – Calgary, Alberta
Ifejika, Samuel U. – Toronto, Ontario
«Indian Rights for Indian Women» – Edmonton, Alberta
«Indo-Canadian Society of Alberta» – Edmonton, Alberta
Info Pop – Montréal, Québec
Innes, Eugene W. – Regina, Saskatchewan
Institut canadien des droits de la personne – Ottawa, Ontario
L'Institut canadien des ingénieurs et ses sociétés constituantes – Montréal, Québec
Institut canadien national des aveugles – Toronto, Ontario
«International Council of Sikhs» – Toronto, Ontario

«The International Ombudsman Institute» – Edmonton,
   Alberta
Ireland, V. – Toronto, Ontario
Irvin, George – Dorchester, Ontario
Ivanochko, Bob – Regina, Saskatchewan
Iwanus, Jaroslaw (Jerry) – Edmonton, Alberta

J

Jackson, Arthur S. – Ottawa, Ontario
Jackson, F. L. – Saint-Jean, Terre-Neuve
Jacob, O. – Oshawa, Ontario
Jaeger, Martin – Toronto, Ontario
James, Norman G. – Burlington, Ontario
Janda, Richard A. – Toronto, Ontario
Jansen, Russell – Kelowna, Colombie-Britannique
Jarionsynski, Witold – Warszawa, Pologne
Jewitt, Brian – Ottawa, Ontario
Jimmie, Sam – Sardis, Colombie-Britannique
Johnson, Calven – Estevan, Saskatchewan
Johnson Chris – Saint-Jean, Nouveau-Brunswick
Johnson, H. S. – Oakville, Ontario
Johnston, Terry L. – Edmonton, Alberta
Johnston, William C. – Burlington, Ontario
Johnstone, D. G. – Hamilton, Ontario
Jones, David G. – Fort McMurray, Alberta
Jones, T. P. – Ottawa, Ontario
Jorlin, Don – Calgary, Alberta
Joynt, C. S. – Calgary, Alberta
Judd, Anne – Port Elgin, Ontario
Julia, Sister M. – London, Ontario
Julian, Glenn E. – Kitchener, Ontario

K

Kabut, Ursula – Brooks, Alberta
Kaiser, K. – Edmonton, Alberta
Kallion, R. – Thunder Bay, Ontario
Kane, Cecce – Salmon Arm, Colombie-Britannique
Kane, Sally – Salmon Arm, Colombie-Britannique
Kay, Roy – New Westminster, Colombie-Britannique
Kear, A. R. – Winnipeg, Manitoba
Keevil, Scott – Oakville, Ontario
Kelly, Allan A. – Thunder Bay, Ontario
Kelly, Margaret – Trout Creek, Ontario
Kelly, Mary – Powassan, Ontario
Kelly, Maureen – London, Ontario
Kemp, Fred D. V. – Calgary, Alberta
Kennedy, Michael P. J. – Saskatoon, Saskatchewan
Kennedy, Sean M. – Montréal, Québec
Kennedy, Jackson, Irlma – Hamilton, Ontario
Kent, Alan – Toronto, Ontario
Kerigan, A. T. – Hamilton, Ontario
Kerr, A. C. (M. et Mme) – Burnaby, Colombie-Britannique

Kerr, Peter – Victoria, Colombie-Britannique
Kerr, Robert W. – Windsor, Ontario
Kieffer, Virginia – Teeswater, Ontario
Kiesman, Clarence – Moosehorn, Manitoba
Killoran, M. Maureen – Hamilton, Ontario
Kim, Mary-Ann – Nepean, Ontario
King, Vivian – Montréal, Québec
Kirton, N. G. – Calgary, Alberta
Kitchen, Kathryn A. – Cambridge, Ontario
Klarer, Allen – Oakville, Ontario
Klein, Ralph – Calgary, Alberta
Klenman, Norman – Vancouver, Colombie-Britannique
Knapp, Bruce H. – Peterborough, Ontario
Knelman, F. H. – Montréal, Québec
«Knights of Columbus (Council 1007)» – North Bay, Ontario
«Knights of Columbus (Council 1916)» – Renfrew, Ontario
«Knights of Columbus (Council 2082)» – Arnprior, Ontario
«Knights of Columbus (Father Doyle Council
    n° 6745)» – Mount Forest, Ontario
«Knights of Columbus (Francis Lemieux Council
    n° 6388)» – Longlac, Ontario
«Knights of Columbus (Marian Council No. 3881)» – Oak-
    ville, Ontario
«Knights of Columbus (Sacred Heart Council 4120)» –
    Tottenham, Ontario
Kocsis, William – Port Stanley, Ontario
Koning, Jean (Mme) – Oldcastle, Ontario
«Kootenay Indian Area Council» – Cranbrook, Colombie-
    Britannique
Korey, George – Toronto, Ontario
Kostuchuk, J. A. – Dauphin, Manitoba
Kowal, Donald – Kingston, Ontario
Kraemer, Anne – Walkerton, Ontario
Kraemer, J. Edward – Walkerton, Ontario
Krenz, Cecil – Saskatoon, Saskatchewan
Kuhn, Bernie – St. Thomas, Ontario
Kulmar, E. – Weston, Ontario
Kumar, Prem – Edmonton, Alberta

L
LaBerge, Dan – Newcastle, Nouveau-Brunswick
La Branche, Richard – Montréal, Québec
«Lac La Biche Chamber of Commerce» – Lac La Biche,
    Alberta
Ladouceur, Yvonne – Montréal, Québec
Lafleur, François – Sainte-Foy, Québec
LaForest, Gérard G. V. – Ottawa, Ontario
«Laichkwitach State Tribes» – Campbell River, Colombie-
    Britannique
Langevin, Celia – Niagara Falls, Ontario
Lapierre, Laurette – Boucherville, Québec
Lapierre, Yvette – Boucherville, Québec

Lapp, M. A. – Calgary, Alberta
La Prairie, Vicki – Aylmer Lucerne, Québec
Larisey, Don – Carleton Place, Ontario
Lauriault, Gary Anthony – Orléans, Ontario
Lavoie, Marie E. – Calgary, Alberta
Laurence, Marilyn L. – Toronto, Ontario
Lawrence, Ross D. – Willowdale, Ontario
Lawson, A. (Mme) – Duchess, Alberta
Lawson, Ina – Thunder Bay, Ontario
«The Law Union of British-Columbia» – Vancouver,
    Colombie-Britannique
Laxdal, Walter V. G. – Saskatoon, Saskatchewan
Layman, Pauline – Victoria, Colombie-Britannique
Leahy, J. H. – Powassan, Ontario
Leblanc, Sylvio – Cornwall, Ontario
LeBreton, Emilien – Lower Neguac, Nouveau-Brunswick
Lécuyer, André – Don Mills, Ontario
Lederman, W. R. – Kingston, Ontario
Lee, John C. – St. Catharines, Ontario
Lee-Paget, D. J. – Winnipeg, Manitoba
Leeder, C. E. – Grimsby, Ontario
Leier, Dale Philip – Lethbridge, Alberta
Leighton, Lynn – Markham, Ontario
Leitch, Pauline D. – Thornhill, Ontario
Lemieux, Joseph-Paul-Émile – Mont-Louis, Comté Gaspé,
    Québec
Lemire, Sister Mary Carol – Willowdale, Ontario
Lentsch, John J. – Delta, Colombie-Britannique
Leon, Robert – Toronto, Ontario
Leuheoct, Biel – Okotoks, Alberta
Levert, J. Raymond – Mississauga, Ontario
Levi, John – Pakenham, Ontario
Leymen, Ken – Vancouver, Colombie-Britannique
Liaison canadienne – Ottawa, Ontario
Lieb, Randy – Swift Current, Saskatchewan
Ligue nationale des Noirs du Canada – Willowdale, Ontario
Ligue protestante canadienne – London, Ontario
Lippect, Frank – Chepston, Ontario
Lipsett, Edward H. – Winnipeg, Manitoba
Little, Nina – Vancouver, Colombie-Britannique
Lockhart, Andy – Calgary, Alberta
Lockwood, Bette – Calgary, Alberta
Logan, Brian James – Edmonton, Alberta
Logan, Lola – Edmonton, Alberta
«London & Middlesex County Roman Catholic Separate
    School Board» – London, Ontario
Long, E. P. M. – Sidney, Colombie-Britannique
Longmore, Elizabeth – Calgary, Alberta
Looyen, C. D. – Surrey, Colombie-Britannique
Looyen, Claire – Surrey, Colombie-Britannique
Lopez, Alicia – St. Thomas, Ontario
Loring, Marian O. – Tangent, Alberta

Lott, David – Ganges, Colombie-Britannique
Loughran, Hugh – Mississauga, Ontario
Loughran, Patricia – Mississauga, Ontario
Love, D. V. – Toronto, Ontario
Lovett, Frank J. (M. et Mme) – Willowdale, Ontario
Lowen, Amy E. – Maple Ridge, Colombie-Britannique
Lower Nicola Band – Merritt, Colombie-Britannique
Lozanski, Walter R. – Calgary, Alberta
Ludlow, Dennis W. – Don Mills, Ontario
Lussier, Michel – Montréal, Québec
Lynch, Mike – St. Thomas, Ontario
Lyon, Noel – Kingston, Ontario
Lyons, Robert – Toronto, Ontario
Lysyk, Kenneth M. – Vancouver, Colombie-Britannique

M
MacKay, A. Wayne – Halifax, Nouvelle-Écosse
MacKenzie, Norma S. – Downsview, North York, Ontario
MacKinnon, J. C. – Saskatoon, Saskatchewan
MacLean, John B. – Kingston, Ontario
MacNeil, Malcolm H. – Frédericton, Nouveau-Brunswick
MacNeill, Dorothy – Port Hawkesbury, Nouvelle-Écosse
Macpherson, Jean (Mme) – Toronto, Ontario
Madden, Wayne D. – Fort McMurray, Alberta
Magee, D. E. – Barrie, Ontario
Mahaffy, Earle F. – Calgary, Alberta
Mahoney, A. P. (Rév.) – London, Ontario
Malloway, Kathy – Sardis, Colombie-Britannique
Malloway, Tony – Sardis, Colombie-Britannique
Maloney, Beverley – Marmora, Ontario
Manis, Vincent – Vancouver, Colombie-Britannique
«Manitoba Association For Rights and Liberties» – Winnipeg,
    Manitoba
«Manitoba Association of Friendship Centres Inc.» –
    Winnipeg, Manitoba
«Manitoba Association of Women and the Law» – Winnipeg,
    Manitoba
«Manitoba Law Union» – Winnipeg, Manitoba
«Manitoba Office of the Ombudsman» – Winnipeg, Manitoba
«Manitoba Parents for Ukrainian Education Inc.» – Winnipeg,
    Manitoba
Mannan, A. – Winnipeg, Manitoba
Mannock, David – Vancouver, Colombie-Britannique
Manor, Robert – Vancouver, Colombie-Britannique
Manson, M. et Mme – Calgary, Alberta
Maoney, Monica – Saint-Jean, Nouveau-Brunswick
Marshall, Hilda A. J. – Victoria, Colombie-Britannique
Martin, L. J. – Calgary, Alberta
Martin, Paul – St. Jacobs, Ontario
Martin, Sandra – Toronto, Ontario
Mascotto, Adrien William – Geraldton, Ontario
Maskell, Fred G. B. – Ottawa, Ontario

Maskell, Monica, M. F. – Ottawa, Ontario
Mason, Clyde D. – Halifax, Nouvelle-Écosse
Mason, Kenneth H. – Dutton, Ontario
Masschaele, James – London, Ontario
Masterson, Brennan F. – Scarborough, Ontario
Maten, Steve – Saint-Bruno, Québec
Matheson, Douglas R. – Edmonton, Alberta
Mathewson, Donald H. – Calgary, Alberta
Matsubara, Mark M. – Ottawa, Ontario
Matte, Louis J. – Prince George, Colombie-Britannique
Matthews, Norman H. – Maple, Ontario
McAllister, Irene L. – Vancouver, Colombie-Britannique
McArthur, D. A. – Guelph, Ontario
McAuley, Daniel L. – Toronto, Ontario
McCaldon, R. J. – Kingston, Ontario
McCall, Gil – Quesnel, Colombie-Britannique
McCamis, J. G. – Calgary, Alberta
McCarthy, Farrell – Newcastle, Nouveau-Brunswick
McCatty, S. A. – Nepean, Ontario
McComb, Albert – Toronto, Ontario
McCormack, Susan – Vancouver, Colombie-Britannique
McCraw, Claire – St. Thomas, Ontario
McCreery, K. J. – Milton, Ontario
McDonald, Robert – Montréal, Québec
McDonald, Virginia – Downsview, Ontario
McDonell, John – Kirkland Lake, Ontario
McDougall, Hugh – Weston, Ontario
McDougall, Gloria – Weston, Ontario
McFadyen, Kevin – Edmonton, Alberta
McFee, Harry F. – Winnipeg, Manitoba
McGillivray, A. B. – Calgary, Alberta
McGirr, James – Brampton, Ontario
McIntosh, Trudy – Sarnia, Ontario
McIntyre, E. – Windsor, Ontario
McIsaac, H. (M. et Mme) – Sudbury, Ontario
McKenzie, Gerald F. – Ajax, Ontario
McKeon, Charles F. – Toronto, Ontario
McKinney, Norman – Toronto, Ontario
McLaughlin, Robert N. – Toronto, Ontario
McLellan, Brian James – Sarnia, Ontario
McLeod, Leona, A. – Victoria, Colombie-Britannique
McLeod, R. A. – Victoria, Colombie-Britannique
McMullen, Norman – Willowdale, Ontario
McNally, Harold – Willowdale, Ontario
McNally, Margaret – Willowdale, Ontario
McNamee, J. J. – New Liskeard, Ontario
McNee, James D. – Brandon, Manitoba
McNulty, Yolande – Oshawa, Ontario
McPhedran, A. – Calgary, Alberta
McRuer, J. C. – Toronto, Ontario
McWhinney, Edward – Vancouver, Colombie-Britannique
Media Club of Canada – Saint-Jean, New Brunswick

«Mennonite Central Committee (Canada)» – Ottawa, Ontario
Mercer, John S. – Toronto, Ontario
Mérey, Pamela – Toronto, Ontario
Mérey, Peter – Toronto, Ontario
«Metis Association of Alberta» – Edmonton, Alberta
«Metropolitan Separate School Board» – Toronto, Ontario
Mewett, Alan W. – Toronto, Ontario
Michalski, C. – Camden East, Ontario
Michalski, W. – Camden East, Ontario
Michaud, Victoria – Powassan, Ontario
Michefske, Martha – Powassan, Ontario
Miles, Robert – Kelowna, Colombie-Britannique
Millar, R. C. – Otterburn Park, Québec
Millen, William – Teeswater, Ontario
Miller, Mary Jane – St. Catharines, Ontario
Miller, Norman W. – Calgary, Alberta
Miller, Wes – Burlington, Ontario
Milner, Betty – Calgary, Alberta
«The Mining Association of Canada» – Ottawa, Ontario
«The Minority Rights Group» – Oakville, Ontario
Miskokoman, Roberta – Muncey, Ontario
Mitchell, Andrew S. – Sidney, Colombie-Britannique
Mitchell, Doris I. – Sault Sainte-Marie, Ontario
Mitchell, Marcelle – Ottawa, Ontario
Mitchell, Osborne – Victoria, Colombie-Britannique
Miyata, T. – Atikokan, Ontario
«Mohawk Council of Kahnawake» – Kahnawake, Québec
Molfora, Giovanni (et groupe) – Montréal, Québec
Moore, J. Sherrold – Calgary, Alberta
Moore, John L. – Vancouver, Colombie-Britannique
Morel, François – Sainte-Foy, Québec
Morgan, David – Halifax, Nouvelle-Écosse
Morgan, W. O. – Vancouver, Colombie-Britannique
Moriarity, Linda – Calgary, Alberta
Morrow, W. R. – Calgary, Alberta
Morton, Ralph – Cowichan Bay, Colombie-Britannique
Mountain, Elizabeth (Beth) – Willowdale, Ontario
Mountain, Howard R. J. – Willowdale, Ontario
Mowers, Cleo W. – Lethbridge, Alberta
Muckle, Marjorie E. – Mississauga, Ontario
Muise, Leonard – Stephenville, Terre-Neuve
«Multicultural Association of Fredericton Inc.» – Frédéricton
    Nouveau-Brunswick
«Multilingual Association of Regina Inc.» – Regina,
    Saskatchewan
Munroe, Isabel A. – Edmonton, Alberta
Murduff, C. (Mme) – Peterborough, Ontario
Murphy, D. P. – Agincourt, Ontario
Murphy, Rhoda – Calgary, Alberta
Murphy, Sandra – St. Thomas, Ontario
Murray, David C. – Guelph, Ontario
Murray, Jim – North Vancouver, Colombie-Britannique

Musial, Frederich A. – Atlin, Colombie-Britannique
Muttart, Margaret W. – Summerside, Île-du-Prince-Édouard

N
NACHES Groupe gai juif de Montréal – Montréal, Québec
Nadeau, Sauveur – Oshawa, Ontario
Nagel, Rudy – Toronto, Ontario
Nalli, Mary – Mississauga, Ontario
Naphin, Robert L. – Saskatoon, Saskatchewan
Nash, David (M. et Mme) – Fort Erie, Ontario
Nassivera, T. (Mme) – Toronto, Ontario
«National Association of Canadians of Origins in India
  (NACOI)» – Ottawa, Ontario
«National Association of Japanese Canadians» – Vancouver,
  Colombie-Britannique
«National Chapter of Canada IODE (Provincial Chapter of
  New Brunswick IODE)» – Toronto, Ontario
«National Citizens' Coalition» – Toronto, Ontario
«National Farmers Union» – Saskatoon, Saskatchewan
«National Firearms Association New Brunswick
  Branch» – Woodstock, Nouveau-Brunswick
«National Indian Brotherhood, Chiefs of Treaty No. 7, Tribes
  of Alberta» – Ottawa, Ontario
«Native Brotherhood of British Columbia» – Vancouver,
  Colombie-Britannique
«Native Peoples Resource Centre» – London, Ontario
«The Native Rights Coalition» – Regina, Saskatchewan
«Native Women's Association of Canada» – Ottawa, Ontario
Nattrass, Eileen – Victoria, Colombie-Britannique
Nederend, Joanne – Breslau, Ontario
Nelson, N. V. – Prince George, Colombie-Britannique
Nelson, Ruben F. W. – Ottawa, Ontario
«Nemiah Valley Band» – Nemiah Valley, Colombie-
  Britannique
«New Brunswick Association for the Advancement of
  Coloured People» – Saint-Jean, Nouveau-Brunswick
«The New Brunswick Development Institute» – Frédéricton,
  Nouveau-Brunswick
«The New Brunswick Human Rights Commission» –
  Frédéricton, Nouveau-Brunswick
Newby, Hester – Niagara Falls, Ontario
«New Democratic Party of Newfoundland & Labrador» –
  Corner Brook, Terre-Neuve
Nichol, Margaret J. – Markham, Ontario
Nicholas, Peter – Trenton, Ontario
Nicholas, S. M. – Calgary, Alberta
Nicholls, Peter – St. Catharines, Ontario
Nicholson, Arthur Gwyn – Orléans, Ontario
Noble, K. W. – Ottawa, Ontario
Nolet, Richard – Sault Sainte-Marie, Ontario
«Nooaitch Indian Reserve» – Meritt, Colombie-Britannique
«North Shore Liberal Women» – West Vancouver,
  Colombie-Britannique

«North Shore Women's Centre» – North Vancouver,
Colombie-Britannique
«The Nova Scotia Network of CCLOW» – Dartmouth,
Nouvelle-Écosse
«Nova Scotia Real Estate Association» – Halifax, Nouvelle-
Écosse
Nowlan, Michel – Ville d'Anjou, Québec

O

Oakley, Elsie – Thamesford, Ontario
O'Brien, Edward – Toronto, Ontario
O'Brien, Margaret – Scarborough, Ontario
O'Connell, William J. – Don Mills, Ontario
O'Connor, Liz – St. Thomas, Ontario
O'Connor, T. Peter – Calgary, Alberta
O'Farrell – Sainte-Foy, Québec
O'Hearn, P. J. T. – Halifax, Nouvelle-Écosse
Ohlheiser, Sandra – Champion, Alberta
Olenick, Roberta – Vancouver, Colombie-Britannique
O'Neill, Mary – Islington, Ontario
«Ontario English Catholic Teachers' Association» – Toronto,
Ontario
«The Ontario Federation of Anglers & Hunters» –
Peterborough, Ontario
«Ontario Human Rights Commission» – Toronto, Ontario
«Ontario Progressive Conservative Association of
Women» – Cornwall, Ontario
«Ontario Separate School Trustees' Association» – Willowdale,
Ontario
«Ontario Welfare Council» – Toronto, Ontario
«Operation Dismantle» – Ottawa, Ontario
Organisation nationale d'anti-pauvreté – Ottawa, Ontario
«Organization for Caribbean Canadian Initiatives» –
Willowdale, Ontario
«Oromocto, Town of» – Oromocto, Nouveau-Brunswick
Orr, A. W. – Calgary, Alberta
O'Shaughnessy, John – Powassan, Ontario
O'Shea, Patrick (M. et Mme) – Rexdale, Ontario
Ottenbrite, K. – Bramalea, Ontario
«Our Lady of the Airways» – Mississauga, Ontario
Owens, Susan – Powassan, Ontario

P

«Pacific Vocational Institute» – Burnaby, Colombie-
Britannique
Palmer, John R. N. – Orillia, Ontario
«Parent Finders Incorporated» – Willowdale, Ontario
Park, Marvin – Canfield, Ontario
Parkman, Cathy – Charlottetown, Île-du-Prince-Édouard
Parti communiste du Canada – Toronto, Ontario
Parti Crédit social de l'Alberta – Alberta
«The Pas Indian Band» – The Pas, Manitoba

Paterson, M. – Calgary, Alberta
Paterson, W. – Calgary, Alberta
Patterson, A. M. – Calgary, Alberta
Patterson, Kathleen A. – West Vancouver, Colombie-Britannique
«Pavilion Indian Band» – Cache Creek, Colombie-Britannique
Pawih, Jack – Cartwright, Manitoba
Payne, Dexter, K. – Kentville, Nouvelle-Écosse
Pearson, George – Lindsay, Ontario
Peel Sharpshooters – Brampton, Ontario
Peet, F. G. – Brentwood Bay, Colombie-Britannique
Pelech, William – Sherwood Park, Alberta
Pelerine, Carolyn – New Glasgow, Nouvelle-Écosse
Penna, Dan E. – Saskatoon, Saskatchewan
Penner, Norman – Toronto, Ontario
«Penticton Indian Band» – Penticton, Colombie-Britannique
«The Peoples Law School Society» – Vancouver, Colombie-Britannique
Pépin, Lorraine – Powassan, Ontario
Perras, P. William jr. – Oakville, Ontario
Perry, Dennis W. – Chester, Nouvelle-Écosse
Perry, Thomas L. jr. – Houston, Colombie-Britannique
«Peterborough Libertarian Association» – Peterborough, Ontario
Peters, Glendon Trevor – Saint-Jean, Nouveau-Brunswick
Petrovici, Boris – St. Catharines, Ontario
Petry, Lucien A. – Regina, Saskatchewan
Pettick, Joseph – Regina, Saskatchewan
Phillips, Wendell – Delta, Colombie-Britannique
Piekarski, Frank – Powassan, Ontario
Piekarski, Teresa – Powassan, Ontario
Piercy, Beth – London, Ontario
Pilisi, Paul – Sainte-Foy, Québec
Pinkney, R. D. – Georgetown, Ontario
Pinsonneault, Rolland – Regina, Saskatchewan
Pitre-Lefebvre, Florence – Saint-Albert, Alberta
Plante, Frank – Windsor, Ontario
Plumley, George – Guelph, Ontario
Podger, Robert J. – Toronto, Ontario
Poechman, Gerald P. – Walkerton, Ontario
Pollock, Nancy – Willowdale, Ontario
Poncelet, Maurice – Ottawa, Ontario
Pope, A. C. – Toronto, Ontario
«The Port Coquitlam Area, Womens Centre» – Port-Coquitlam, Colombie-Britannique
Porteous, James – Willowdale, Ontario
Porter, H. A. – Ottawa, Ontario
Porter, K. E. – Winnipeg, Manitoba
«Port Simpson Band Council» – Port Simpson, Colombie-Britannique
«Positive Action Committee» – Montréal, Québec
Poulin, Gaétan – Saint-Agapit, Québec

«The Presbytery of Newfoundland» – Saint-Jean, Terre-Neuve
«Prescott-Russell County Roman Catholic Separate School
   Board» – L'Orignal, Ontario
Prest, Steve – Sardis, Colombie-Britannique
Pringle, W. R. – Winnipeg, Manitoba
«Progressive Conservative Women's Association of
   North-Bay» – North Bay, Ontario
«Progressive Conservative Party of Saskatchewan» –
   Saskatchewan
«Progressive Conservative Association of Okanagan North» –
   Kelowna, Colombie-Britannique
«Provincial Association of Catholic Teachers» – Montréal,
   Québec
«Provincial Progressive Conservative Association» – Calgary,
   Alberta
Puddy, James et Margaret – Agincourt, Ontario
«Public Interest Advocacy Centre» – Ottawa, Ontario

Q
Quarry, Grace, Andrew and Robert George – Guelph, Ontario
«Quebec Federation of Home and School Associations» –
   Montréal, Québec
«Quebecer's Labrador Association» – Les Grondines, Québec
Quesnel, Janine – Crysler, Ontario
Quigley, Robert F. – Saint-Jean, Terre-Neuve
Quitner, Joe K. – Toronto, Ontario

R
Ragona, Linda – Calgary, Alberta
Rastall, Peter – Vancouver, Colombie-Britannique
Rauser, John – Mitchell, Ontario
«Realty Owners of Canada» – Don Mills, Ontario
Recluses Missionnaires – Montréal, Québec
«Red Pheasant Band, No. 108» – Cando, Saskatchewan
«Redemptorist Fathers» – Toronto, Ontario
Reed, Lorne H. – Calgary, Alberta
Regehr, Echo – Coutts, Alberta
Regehr, Jack – Coutts, Alberta
Le Regroupement pour les droits politiques du Québec –
   Montréal, Québec
Reichert, Walter – Pilger, Saskatchewan
Reid, John S. – Cambridge, Ontario
Reinke, H. S. – Thornhill, Ontario
«Religious Information Centre» – Vancouver, Colombie-
   Britannique
«The Religious Society of Friends (Quaker)» – Saint-Jean,
   Terre-Neuve
Rémillard, Gil – Montréal, Québec
«Renaissance Family Institute» – Milton, Ontario
Renaissance International – Milton, Ontario
Renaud, J.-Claude – Gatineau, Québec
Renault, Arlene M. – Salmon Arm, Colombie-Britannique
Richard, Ethel – Ottawa, Ontario

Rick, Alban – Powassan, Ontario
Rick, Louise – Powassan, Ontario
«Right to Life» – Kitchener, Ontario
«Right to Life Association of Toronto and Area» – Toronto, Ontario
Riley, K. E. – Lethbridge, Alberta
Rinck, Aksel – Weston, Ontario
Ring, Harold et Winifred – Richmond Hill, Ontario
Ringrose, E. G. – Calgary, Alberta
Ritchie, H. S. – Stratford, Ontario
Robertson, Elizabeth – Didsbury, Alberta
Robertson, H. – Stratford, Ontario
Robinson, Sharon – Edmonton, Alberta
Rodwick, Graeme – Nepean, Ontario
Rogers, Craig T. – Windsor, Ontario
Rogers, Elwyn A. – Toronto, Ontario
Rogers, Smellard, Jane Daphne – Peterborough, Ontario
Rombough, Jessie – Calgary, Alberta
Ronaghan, Allan – Winnipeg, Manitoba
Roper, Henry – Halifax, Nouvelle-Écosse
Rosenberg, Richard S. – Winnipeg, Manitoba
Ross, Romaine K. – St. Catharines, Ontario
Rossi, Carlo – Ottawa, Ontario
Rothney, Gordon – St. John College, Manitoba
Roussel, Georges – Oshawa, Ontario
Routliffe, C. D. – Mississauga, Ontario
Rowe, F. W. – Ottawa, Ontario
Roxan, Ian – Toronto, Ontario
Roy, Albert J. – Ottawa, Ontario
Roy, Gilles & Desneiges – Southampton, Ontario
«The Royal Commonwealth Society» – Toronto, Ontario
Rowe, Elizabeth – London, Ontario
Rudd, Theodore – Lethbridge, Alberta
Rudnyckyj, J. B. – Montréal, Québec
Rudolph, Mildred – Lloydminster, Alberta
Ruffman, Alan – Halifax, Nouvelle-Écosse
Rundle, B. J. – Toronto, Ontario
Rurak, George – Salmon Arm, Colombie-Britannique
Russell, Hubert E. – Islington, Ontario
Russell, Peter H. – Toronto, Ontario
Rutledge, Douglas E. – Belleville, Ontario
Rutledge, Fred – Moncton, Nouveau-Brunswick
Ryan, H.R.S. – Kingston, Ontario

S
«St. Andrew's College in Winnipeg» – Winnipeg, Manitoba
«St. Boniface Catholic Women's League of Canada» – Maryhill, Ontario
«St. Clare School» – Mississauga, Ontario
«St. Mary's Band» – Cranbrook, Colombie-Britannique
«All Saints' Anglican Church» – Milville, Saskatchewan
Saldov, Morris – Toronto, Ontario

Sallmen, Helen – Ottawa, Ontario
Bande Salteau n° 542 – East Moberly Lake, Colombie-
Britannique
Sam, Mitze – Vedder Crossing, Colombie-Britannique
Sander, Joe – Saskatoon, Saskatchewan
Sander, Roy – Vauxhall, Alberta
Sanders, Douglas – Vancouver, Colombie-Britannique
Saprarolle, Gertrude – Saskatoon, Saskatchewan
«Sarnia Indian Research» – Sarnia, Ontario
«Saskatchewan Advisory Council on the Status of Women» –
Saskatoon, Saskatchewan
«Saskatchewan Human Rights Commission» – Saskatoon,
Saskatchewan
«Saskatchewan Real Estate Association» – Saskatoon,
Saskatchewan
«Saskatoon Catholic Schools» – Saskatoon, Saskatchewan
Say, Vivian I. – Vancouver, Colombie-Britannique
Sayer, Laurie – London, Ontario
Schelvey, M. A. – London, Ontario
Schmalz, Alice – Cambridge, Ontario
«School Sisters of Notre-Dame» – Waterdown, Ontario
Schuetz, C. F. – Ottawa, Ontario
Schurter, Jerome – Chepstow, Ontario
Schwartz, Bryan – Ottawa, Ontario
Scott, Donald A. – Winnipeg, Manitoba
Scott, Jackie – Cupar, Saskatchewan
Scott, Len – Cupar, Saskatchewan
Scott, Stephen A. – Westmount, Québec
«Scowlitz Indian Band» – Harrison Mills, Colombie-
Britannique
Secor Inc. – Montréal, Québec
Seguin, Sweeney Denise – London, Ontario
Seidl, Peter – Vancouver, Colombie-Britannique
«Senior Citizens' Central Council of Calgary» – Calgary,
Alberta
Sepass, Mona – Sardis, Colombie-Britannique
Seto, David – Chicoutimi, Québec
«Shackan Indian Band» – Merritt, Colombie-Britannique
Shaw, M. A. – Calgary, Alberta
Shea, Patrick D. – Ottawa, Ontario
Shead, Bill – Selkirk, Manitoba
Shore, Martin – Victoria, Colombie-Britannique
Short, Leslie – Montréal, Québec
Siddon, T. – Richmond, Colombie-Britannique
Silaj, Les – Elliot, Colombie-Britannique
Silver, Shoel – Toronto, Ontario
Simpson, C. H. – Kelowna, Colombie-Britannique
Simpson, W. E. – Belleville, Ontario
Sims, Anthony
Sinclair, E. Jean – Vancouver, Colombie-Britannique
Sinclair, L. R. – Vancouver, Colombie-Britannique
Sinclair, Stanley R. – Regina, Saskatchewan

Sindlinger, Tom – Edmonton, Alberta
Slattery, Brian – Saskatoon, Saskatchewan
«Slovenian Canadian Association» – Edmonton, Alberta
Smed, John – Calgary, Alberta
Smeele, Stan J. – Victoria, Colombie-Britannique
Smiley, Donald – Downsview Ontario
Smiley, Harold – Enderby, Colombie-Britannique
Smiley, Lillian – Salmon Arm, Colombie-Britannique
Smith, Anne – Timmins, Ontario
Smith, David P. – Ottawa, Ontario
Smith, Denis – Peterborough, Ontario
Smith, Denis – Toronto, Ontario
Smith, Dolina – Scarborough, Ontario
Smith, Edgar A. – Willowdale, Ontario
Smith, George – Winona, Ontario
Smith, Gery, R. C. – Brockville, Ontario
Smith, Jean M. – Keswick, Ontario
Smith, Lillian et Don – Concord, Ontario
Smith, Marion – Windsor, Ontario
Smith, Zeta – Winona, Ontario
Smoke, Lapierre, Arthur – Willowdale, Ontario
Snook, Earl F. – North Vancouver, Colombie-Britannique
«The Social Credit Party of Alberta» – Alberta
«Social Credit Party of Canada» – Montréal, Québec
«Social Planning and Review Council of British Columbia» –
    Vancouver, Colombie-Britannique
La Société des Acadiens du Nouveau-Brunswick – Moncton,
    Nouveau-Brunswick
Société franco-manitobaine – Saint-Boniface, Manitoba
Société nationale des Québécois des Cantons de
    l'Est – Coaticook, Québec
La Société Saint-Jean Baptiste de la Mauricie –
    Trois-Rivières, Québec
Société Saint-Jean Baptiste de Montréal – Montréal, Québec
Société Saint-Jean Baptiste de Québec – Québec, Québec
Sœurs de l'Assomption de la Sainte-Vierge de Nicolet –
    Nicolet, Québec
Les Sœurs de Notre-Dame du perpétuel secours – Saint-
    Damien, Bellechasse, Québec
«Search The Society for Education, Action, Research and
    Counselling on Homosexuality» – Vancouver, Colombie-
    Britannique
Soltermann, J. – Medicine Hat, Alberta
Somcynsky, Thomas – Sherbrooke, Québec
Sommerville, R. J. – Peterborough, Ontario
«South Central Tribal Council» – Kamloops, Colombie-
    Britannique
«South Okanagan Civil Liberties Society» – Penticton,
    Colombie-Britannique
«Southwestern Ontario Campaign Life» – St. George, Ontario
Soward, S. E. – Victoria, Colombie-Britannique
«Spallumcheen Band» – Enderby, Colombie-Britannique

Sparks, Ann – Calgary, Alberta
Spinney, Robert E. – Calgary, Alberta
Splane, Richard B. – Ottawa, Ontario
Stallard, Sidney – New Glasgow, Nouvelle-Écosse
Stang, Egbert – Saskatoon, Saskatchewan
Stanton, Michael S. – Calgary, Alberta
Steer, Gary – St. Thomas, Ontario
Stelter, Alice, Wayne – Edmonton, Alberta
Stephens, John V. – Toronto, Ontario
Stevenson, J. G. A. – North Bay, Ontario
Stevenson, S. – London, Ontario
Stewart, E. – Calgary, Alberta
Summer, Audrey – Maple Ridge, Colombie-Britannique
Sumpton, James M. – Vancouver, Colombie-Britannique
«Surrey-White Rock Right to Choose Society» – Surrey-White
    Rock, Colombie-Britannique
Swift, W. H. – Edmonton, Alberta

T
Tafel, R. D. – North Bay, Ontario
Tait, Janice – Ottawa, Ontario
Tait, Lyal – Port Burwell, Ontario
Tanguay, André – Oshawa, Ontario
Tates, Irene – Kamloops, Colombie-Britannique
Taylor, James C. – Toronto, Ontario
Teme-Augama Anishnaboi – Lake Temagami, Ontario
The Poet, John – Chatham, Ontario
Tennant, W. – Kamloops, Colombie-Britannique
Tholenau, Carol – Calgary, Alberta
Thomas, Dale – Thamesville, Ontario
Thomas, Eugene – Toronto, Ontario
Thompson, Andrew – Vancouver, Colombie-Britannique
Thompson, Cara M. – Barrie, Ontario
Thompson, Daniel L. – Saint-Jean, Terre-Neuve
Thompson, Edith – Richmond, Colombie-Britannique
Thompson, Ruby M. – Wolfville, Nouvelle-Écosse
«Thunder Bay Multicultural Association» – Thunder Bay,
    Ontario
Tiffin, V. R. – Victoria, Colombie-Britannique
Timmer, F. J. – Kitchener, Ontario
Timmins, Edward et Colleen – Pickering, Ontario
Todres, Irving – Montréal, Québec
Tomar, Mukhtyae S. – Dartmouth, Nouvelle-Écosse
Toosey Band – Williams Lake, Colombie-Britannique
Tophom, Reg et Barb – Powassan, Ontario
Toporoski, R. M. – Toronto, Ontario
Torok, Stephen – Timmins, Ontario
«The Toronto and Montreal Committee to Defend Quebec's
    Right to Self-Determination» – Mississauga, Ontario
«The Toronto Elizabeth Fry Society» – Toronto, Ontario
Tremblay, D. M. – London, Ontario
Tremblay, Peter A. – Sardis, Colombie-Britannique

Trethewey, A. – Kingston, Ontario
Trittler, Mauria – St. Thomas, Ontario
Trotlier, Colette – St. Thomas, Ontario
Turnbull, M. – Calgary, Alberta
Turner, Jim – Prince Albert, Saskatchewan

U

«Ukrainian Canadian Committee» – Winnipeg, Manitoba
«Ukrainian Greek Orthodox Church of Canada» – Edmonton,
    Alberta
L'Union culturelle des franco-ontariennes – L'Orignal,
    Ontario
«Union of British Columbia Indian Chiefs» – Vancouver,
    Colombie-Britannique
«Union of British Columbia Municipalities» –
    New Westminster, Colombie-Britannique
Union nationale – Québec, Québec
«Union of New Brunswick Indians» – Frédéricton, Nouveau-
    Brunswick
«Union of Nova Scotia Indians» – Sydney, Nouvelle-Écosse
«The Union of Ontario Indians» – Toronto, Ontario
Union populaire – Charlesbourg, Québec
«The United Church of Canada» – Edmonton, Alberta
«United Church of Canada» – Montréal, Québec
«The United Church of Canada» – Saint-Jean, Terre-Neuve
«The United Church of Canada» – Truro, Nouvelle-Écosse
«The United Church of Canada» – Toronto, Ontario
«The United Church of Canada» – Welland, Ontario
«United Hungarian Fund» – Toronto, Ontario
«United Native Nations Society» – Vancouver, Colombie-
    Britannique
«The University Women's Club of Barrie» – Barrie, Ontario
«The University of British Columbia (Members of the History
    420)»: Doug, Archer; Hayward, Ann; Braisto, Colin;
    Keelan, Mark; Gee, Richard; Leonard, Sandra; Greenword,
    F. M.; Seidl, Peter; Wolf, Murray – Vancouver,
    Colombie-Britannique
«The University Women's Club of North York» – Toronto,
    Ontario
«The University Women's Club of White Rock» – White Rock,
    Colombie-Britannique
«Upper Nicola Indian Band» – Merritt, Colombie-Britannique
Usher, Dan – Kingston, Ontario

V

«Vancouver Community Legal Assistance Society» –
    Vancouver, Colombie-Britannique
«The Vancouver Multicultural Society» – Vancouver,
    Colombie-Britannique
«Vancouver Quadra Progressive Conservative Association» –
    Vancouver, Colombie-Britannique

«Vancouver Status of Women» – Vancouver, Colombie-Britannique

Van Dom, Gerald – Mississauga, Ontario

Vanden, Bernard E. – Ottawa, Ontario

Vanderwood, Sandra et Jack – Okanagan, Colombie-Britannique

Van der Wal Hylke – Via La Loche, Saskatchewan

Van Dusen John – Weston, Ontario

Van Koughnet, Edward – Kinsington, Île-du-Prince-Édouard

Van Mierlo, J. B. – Powassan, Ontario

Vasa Order of American, Grand Lodge – Edmonton, Alberta

Verrall, Catherine – Hamilton, Ontario

Verreau, David, Albert, John – Edmonton, Alberta

Vickers, Herb – Calgary, Alberta

Ville de Saint-Nicolas – Saint-Nicolas, Comté de Lévis, Québec

Voelker, Erwin – Chomedy/Laval, Québec

Voice for Life – Wingham, Ontario

«Voice of Women» – Toronto, Ontario

«Voluntary Resource Council» – Charlottetown, Île-du-Prince-Édouard

W

Woechter, Len – Walkerton, Ontario

Wagner, Frank – Toronto, Ontario

Walker, H. K. – Guelph, Ontario

Walker, Marjorie E. – Guelph, Ontario

Walker, Reagan D. – Mississauga, Ontario

Wallace, Donald C. – Downsview, Ontario

Walsh, James F. – Saint-Jean, Terre-Neuve

Warby, Marney – Hamilton, Ontario

Wardle, Thomas A. – Toronto, Ontario

Warner, J. E. – Hamilton, Ontario

Wasteneys, Geoffrey – Ottawa, Ontario

Waterloo Chronicle – Waterloo, Ontario

Watson, Geoffrey – Picton, Ontario

Watson, John R. – North Battleford, Saskatchewan

Watt, Leonard, J. – Calgary, Alberta

Wawryshyn, Michael – Toronto, Ontario

Way, J. (M. et Mme) – Powassan, Ontario

Weaver, Monna – Vancouver, Colombie-Britannique

Webb, George – Ilderton, Ontario

Weber, Milton – Vancouver, Colombie-Britannique

Weidinger, Regince – Cambridge, Ontario

Weiss, Dan – Formosa, Ontario

Wendland, Jack – Maryhill, Ontario

Westbury, Richard S. – Calgary, Alberta

«Western Federation Society» – Victoria, Colombie-Britannique

«West Fed Association of Alberta» – Edmonton, Alberta

Wettlaufer, Bernice – Weston, Ontario

Weygang, Peter – Kenora, Ontario

Whitby, Percy – Sudbury, Ontario

White, Frank – Victoria, Colombie-Britannique

«White Rock University Women» – Surrey, Colombie-
Britannique

Wicklum, Earle L. – Weston, Ontario

Wilbur, Keith – Windsor, Ontario

Wildfong, Marjorie – Cambridge, Ontario

Wildsmith, Bruce H. – Halifax, Nouvelle-Écosse

Willems, Frank – North Battleford, Saskatchewan

Williams, B. M. – Darthmouth, Nouvelle-Écosse

Williams, Paul W. – Ladysmith, Colombie-Britannique

Williams, Peter H. – Toronto, Ontario

Williams, Richard – Chilliwack, Colombie-Britannique

Williams, S. A. – Ottawa, Ontario

Willis, S. D. – Alliston, Ontario

Wilson, Sam – Cayaga, Ontario

Winslow, Edward T. – West Vancouver, Colombie-
Britannique

Winsor, William D. – Saint-Jean, Terre-Neuve

Witchell, John B. – Pierrefonds, Québec

Wittke, Millie – Eganville, Ontario

Wodiuk, William – Toronto, Ontario

Woehrling, José – Montréal, Québec

Woledge, Jack O. – Jasper, Alberta

«Women's Action Committee for Human Rights» – Kitchener,
Ontario

«Women's Habitat» – Etobicoke, Ontario

«Women's Research Centre» – Vancouver, Colombie-
Britannique

«Women for Political Action» – Toronto, Ontario

Wood, Sharon – Alderson, Ontario

Woods, George Beatty – Don Mills, Ontario

Woodward, Helen E. – Mississauga, Ontario

Wright, Bill – Calgary, Alberta

Wright, Cathryn – Wallaceburg, Ontario

Wright, Gerald K. – Duncan, Colombie-Britannique

Wright, N. A. – Weston, Ontario

Wyman, Max – Edmonton, Alberta

Wyme, J. C. – Calgary, Alberta

Wynne, Hildburg S. – Ottawa, Ontario

Y

Yalden, Maxwell F. – Ottawa, Ontario

Yarie, Dale M. – Moose Jaw, Saskatchewan

Yeoman, Mark M. – Dorchester, Nouveau-Brunswick

Yetman, R. H. – Calgary, Alberta

Young, Michael – Don Mills, Ontario

«Young Women's Christian Association of Canada» – Toronto,
Ontario

«Young Women's Christian Association of Canada» – Calgary,
Alberta

Younger, J. W. – Toronto, Ontario

«Yukon Advisory Council» – Whitehorse, Yukon
Yurko, William J. – Edmonton, Alberta
Yuzda, Laurence W. – Calgary, Alberta

Z
Zarubin, George – Yorkton, Saskatchewan
ZoBell, Bob M. – Raymond, Alberta
Zurawell, Anthony – Oshawa, Ontario

Y

Yalden, Maxwell F. – Ottawa, Ontario

Yarie, Dale M. – Moose Jaw, Saskatchewan

Yeoman, Mark M. – Dorchester, New Brunswick

Yetman, R. H. – Calgary, Alberta

Young, Michael – Don Mills, Ontario

Young Women's Christian Association of Canada – Toronto, Ontario

Young Women's Christian Association of Canada – Calgary, Alberta

Younger, J. W. – Toronto, Ontario

Yukon Advisory Council – Whitehorse, Yukon

Yurko, William J. – Edmonton, Alberta

Yuzda, Lawrence W. – Calgary, Alberta

Z

Zarubin, George – Yorkton, Saskatchewan

ZoBell, Bob M. – Raymond, Alberta

Zurawell, Anthony – Oshawa, Ontario

This document has been published to increase understanding of the Canadian Charter of Rights and Freedoms and to heighten awareness of its significance in our daily lives.

This publication is not a legal document. The notes in the booklet are for explanatory purposes only, and are not to be taken as legal interpretations of the provisions of the Charter.

Additional copies of this booklet may be obtained by writing to:

> Publications Canada
> P. O. Box 1986
> Station B
> Ottawa, Canada
> K1P 6G6

27(4-82)

The Charter
of Rights
and Freedoms

A Guide
for
Canadians

Canada

Foreword

When future generations of Canadians look back on what we accomplished in 1981, I am sure they will be proud of the new chapter we have added to the history of this country.

As contemporary Canadians we have been witnessing and participating in truly historic events leading up to Canada's "coming of age," as it were. We have reached at last the goal of that long journey to full, sovereign independence that began with Confederation in 1867.

It hasn't always been an easy journey. But then the Fathers of Confederation knew they were facing formidable obstacles in their effort to create a new nation in the northern half of North America. In the years since, Canadians have shown themselves equal to the challenges and more than capable of overcoming the obstacles.

Now the Parliament of Canada, in the name of all Canadians, has acted to bring the country's Constitution home where it belongs. What this means is that we will never again have to go to the Parliament of another country to ask for changes that we, as Canadians, want to make in our most fundamental law.

The Parliamentary resolution that sets out the details of our truly Canadian Constitution is important to every citizen, containing as it does many of the long-established provisions that form the foundations of our society and of the laws under which we conduct our affairs.

But in the day-to-day lives of Canadians, probably the most significant feature of our Constitution is a new one – the Canadian Charter of Rights and Freedoms.

Most of the rights and freedoms we are enshrining in the Charter are not *totally* new and different. Indeed, Canadians have tended to take most of them for granted over the years. The difference is that now they will be guaranteed by our Constitution, and people will have the power to appeal to the courts if they feel their constitutional rights have been infringed upon or denied.

If the long and searching public debate leading up to patriation of the Constitution proved nothing else, it proved that Canadians need and want their rights and freedoms protected. Enshrining these rights in our Constitution is an essential part of that process.

We may find in the future that we want to improve and refine the Charter of Rights and Freedoms, to strengthen the protection it provides for all our people.

With our own Constitution home in Canada, we are able to make those kinds of changes, as we see fit. We will do it by working together with all the partners in our federation, in the spirit of those who worked together for more than a century to make Canada a free and bountiful land.

Pierre Elliott Trudeau
Prime Minister of Canada

Preface

In a free and democratic society, it is important that citizens know exactly what their rights and freedoms are, and where to turn to for help and advice in the event that those freedoms are denied or rights infringed upon. In a country like Canada – vast and diverse, with 11 governments, two official languages and a variety of ethnic origins – the only way to provide equal protection to everyone is to enshrine those basic rights and freedoms in the Constitution.

Now, for the first time, we will have a Canadian Charter of Rights and Freedoms that recognizes certain rights for all of us, wherever we may live in Canada.

To be sure, there has been a host of federal and provincial laws guaranteeing some of our fundamental rights and freedoms. However, these laws have varied from province to province, with the result that basic rights have been unevenly protected throughout our country. Now that our rights will be written into the Constitution, it will be a constant reminder to our political leaders that they must wield their authority with caution and wisdom.

In October of 1980, the Government of Canada placed before Parliament a proposed Resolution respecting the Constitution of Canada, which included a Charter of Rights and Freedoms. After debate in the House of Commons and the Senate, a Special Joint Committee consisting of members of both Houses of Parliament was established to study the proposed Resolution.

The Special Joint Committee heard from some 300 witnesses speaking for about 100 groups from all parts of Canada. In addition, it received a large number of constructive written submissions.

The Government of Canada studied with great care both the written briefs and the oral testimony of all the witnesses and, taking into account the points made by the members of the Special Joint Committee, over 70 major changes were made to the proposed Resolution.

More debate followed in Parliament. Then in September 1981, the Supreme Court of Canada ruled that the government and Parliament of Canada were within their legal rights to proceed, although it also stated that the federal action was not in accordance with constitutional convention.

Following that ruling, the Prime Minister and the provincial premiers returned to the bargaining table in early November, and reached the consensus that had eluded Canadian governments for decades.

This publication has been prepared to help you better understand the Canadian Charter of Rights and Freedoms. If you need further information or if you feel that your rights have been infringed upon, remember that your Member of Parliament or your Member of the provincial Legislative Assembly is available to help you. Various federal agencies also offer assistance. A list of these agencies and their addresses appears at the end of this publication.

Jean Chrétien
Minister of Justice

Contents

Constitution Act, 1982*

PART I
Canadian Charter of Rights and Freedoms

Whereas Canada is founded upon principles that recognize the supremacy of God and the rule of law:

Guarantee of Rights and Freedoms

1. The *Canadian Charter of Rights and Freedoms* guarantees the rights and freedoms set out in it subject only to such reasonable limits prescribed by law as can be demonstrably justified in a free and democratic society.

"This measure that I introduce is the first step on the part of Canada to carry out the acceptance either of the international declaration of human rights or of the principles that actuated those who produced that noble document."

The Right Honourable John G. Diefenbaker, Canadian Bill of Rights, House of Commons, July 1, 1960

"Canadians could take no more meaningful step than to entrench firmly in our Constitution those fundamental rights and liberties which we possess and cherish."

The Right Honourable Lester B. Pearson, Introduction, Federalism for the Future, Ottawa, January 1968

"We must now establish the basic principles, the basic values and beliefs which hold us together as Canadians so that beyond our regional loyalties there is a way of life and a system of values which make us proud of the country that has given us such freedom and such immeasurable joy."

The Right Honourable Pierre Elliott Trudeau, 1981

---

* The resolution as passed by the Canadian Parliament in December, 1981, referred to the Constitution Act, 1981. However, when the legislation is passed by the British Parliament, it will become the Constitution Act, 1982.

Explanation

This part of the *Constitution Act, 1982*, sets out a Canadian Charter of Rights and Freedoms that establishes for all Canadians protection of certain basic rights and freedoms essential to maintaining our free and democratic society and a united country.

This Charter of Rights applies to all governments – federal, provincial and territorial – and will provide protection of the following:
- fundamental freedoms
- democratic rights
- the right to live and to seek employment anywhere in Canada
- legal rights
- equality rights for all individuals
- official languages of Canada
- minority language education rights
- Canada's multicultural heritage
- native people's rights

Canadians have enjoyed many of these basic rights and freedoms as a matter of practice for many years. Certain rights were set out in the *Canadian Bill of Rights*, which was introduced by Prime Minister John G. Diefenbaker in 1960, as well as in various provincial laws. However, including them in a Charter of Rights, written into the Constitution, will clarify and strengthen them.

At the same time, though, in a democratic society, rights cannot be absolute; they must be qualified in order to protect the rights of others. For instance, freedom of speech must be qualified by libel and slander laws. Therefore this section will allow that the rights that the Charter guarantees will be subject to such limitations as are shown to be justified in a free and democratic society.

Certain Charter rights are subject to another kind of limitation. Fundamental freedoms, legal rights and equality rights could be subject to a "notwithstanding clause." This means that Parliament or a provincial legislature could pass legislation that conflicts with a

Fundamental Freedoms

2. Everyone has the following fundamental freedoms:
  (*a*) **freedom of conscience and religion;**
  (*b*) **freedom of thought, belief, opinion and expression, including freedom of the press and other media of communication;**
  (*c*) **freedom of peaceful assembly; and**
  (*d*) **freedom of association.**

"I share the commitment of many in this House and in this country to a very strong charter of rights..."

The Right Honourable Joe Clark, Leader of the Opposition, House of Commons, February 23, 1981

3

specific provision of the Charter in one of those areas.
Any such legislation would expire after five years unless
specifically renewed. The value of this clause is that it
will ensure that legislatures rather than judges have the
final say on important matters of public policy. The
provision will allow unforeseen situations to be corrected
without the need for constitutional amendment.

The Charter enshrines certain fundamental freedoms for
everyone in Canada. They are freedoms that custom and
law over the years have made almost universal in our
country. Now these freedoms will be protected by the
Constitution.

As Canadians, we are guaranteed the right to worship,
or not, as we wish, in the place of worship of our choice.
Freedom of the press and other media is ensured and
our right to gather in peaceful groups as well as our
right to freedom of association is protected.

Democratic Rights

Democratic
rights of
citizens

3. Every citizen of Canada has the right to vote in an election of members of the House of Commons or of a legislative assembly and to be qualified for membership therein.

Maximum
duration of
legislative
bodies

4. (1) No House of Commons and no legislative assembly shall continue for longer than five years from the date fixed for the return of the writs at a general election of its members.

Continuation
in special
circumstances

(2) In time of real or apprehended war, invasion or insurrection, a House of Commons may be continued by Parliament and a legislative assembly may be continued by the legislature beyond five years if such continuation is not opposed by the votes of more than one-third of the members of the House of Commons or the legislative assembly, as the case may be.

Even though we have, over the years, tended to take our rights for granted, there have been cases in Canada where some fundamental rights have been denied by laws of government.

For example, in 1937 the Alberta Legislature passed a law that would have required newspapers to reveal their sources of news and to publish without charge "information" supplied by the government. In 1937, the Quebec government's "padlock law" banned the propagation of Communism and Bolshevism by closing up and padlocking any premises used for those purposes. In the early 1950s a Quebec City bylaw, passed under the Charter of the City of Quebec, prohibited the distribution in the streets of any book, pamphlet or tract without permission of the chief of police. To Jehovah's Witnesses, the bylaw was a restriction of their rights as Canadian citizens to freedom of expression and freedom of religious practice.

The tradition of democratic rights in Canada is specifically guaranteed by the Charter. Citizens will have a constitutionally enshrined right to vote in elections for members of the House of Commons or a legislative assembly and to seek election to either of those houses.

The only restrictions that may be placed on your right to vote or run in an election will be those that are considered to be reasonable and justified, such as the age restriction for minors, mental incompetence, and certain restrictions on some election officials, such as returning officers, who may have to cast a deciding ballot. In the case of seeking elective office there may be some restrictions on judges because of the non-partisan nature of their office.

It is a well-established principle in a democracy that governments cannot continue their hold on power indefinitely without asking the voters for a new mandate. Now

5. There shall be a sitting of Parliament and of each legislature at least once every twelve months.

"Any legislature can prolong its own life for as long as it sees fit. The legislature of Manitoba prolonged its own life for a few months in 1908. The legislature of Ontario did the same in 1918 until after the return of the soldiers from overseas and again, for a year, in 1942, and again for the same period in 1943. In Saskatchewan in 1943 there was vigorous opposition, but the legislature extended its life for a year."

Senator Eugene Forsey, 1979, How Canadians Govern Themselves

Mobility Rights

Mobility of
citizens

6. (1) Every citizen of Canada has the right to enter, remain in and leave Canada.

Rights to
move and gain
livelihood

(2) Every citizen of Canada and every person who has the status of a permanent resident of Canada has the right
(*a*) to move to and take up residence in any province; and
(*b*) to pursue the gaining of a livelihood in any province.

Limitation

(3) The rights specified in subsection (2) are subject to
(*a*) any laws or practices of general application in force in a province other than those that discriminate among persons primarily on the basis of province of present or previous residence; and

7

the principle will be enshrined in law, in a section of the Charter that says no Parliament or provincial legislative assembly shall continue for more than five years, except in very extraordinary circumstances, such as war, insurrection or invasion. Even then, continuing the life of an elected assembly would be possible only with the approval of two-thirds of the members of Parliament or the legislature concerned.

The Charter will also provide that there must be a sitting of Parliament and each provincial legislature at least once every 12 months so that the government remains accountable to the elected members. This annual sitting rule for the federal Parliament is already covered by the *BNA Act*. However, previously there was no similar constitutionally entrenched rule for the provinces.

This section will provide that Canadians are free to enter, remain in, or leave Canada. An example of government interfering with mobility rights is the treatment of the Japanese-Canadians during, and after, World War II. In the early 1940s, cabinet issued an order under the authority of the War Measures Act which stripped them of their citizenship.

Mobility rights give all Canadian citizens and permanent residents the right to live and seek employment anywhere in Canada. For most of the years since Confederation in 1867, Canadians have assumed these rights existed and in fact exercised them, but never before were they guaranteed in our Constitution.

The mobility guarantee means that you will be able to move to any province or territory from any other, without hindrance, and look for work there. Or, you will be

(*b*) any laws providing for reasonable residency requirements as a qualification for the receipt of publicly provided social services.

Affirmative action programs

(4) Subsections (2) and (3) do not preclude any law, program or activity that has as its object the amelioration in a province of conditions of individuals in that province who are socially or economically disadvantaged if the rate of employment in that province is below the rate of employment in Canada.

". . . But here, where we are one country and all together, and we go from one province to another as we do from one county to another and from one town to another . . ."

Sir John A. Macdonald, House of Commons Debates, 1882

"In this respect, I find it difficult to take seriously any concern that entrenching in our Constitution the right of people to live and work anywhere in Canada could frustrate legitimate provincial objectives. Indeed, it is my hope that some day it will be beyond the reach of government to discriminate against the free movement of services as well."

Honourable William Davis, Premier of Ontario, Financial Post Conference, Toronto, February 26, 1981

Legal Rights

Life, liberty and security of person

7. Everyone has the right to life, liberty and security of the person and the right not to be deprived thereof except in accordance with the principles of fundamental justice.

able to live in one province and pursue the gaining of your livelihood in another. No general restrictions may be placed on you just because you come from another part of the country. However, this will not prohibit the provinces from setting residence requirements for certain social and welfare benefits existing in the provinces. Moreover, the ordinary rules of employment in the province will apply to newcomers the same as to long-time residents. These could include qualifications, union membership, experience, health and so on, providing these applied equally to residents and to people coming from outside the province.

However, a province in which the employment rate is below the national average will have the right to undertake affirmative action programs for socially and economically disadvantaged individuals.

It is interesting to note that Canadians have been highly mobile in recent years. During the year from October 1979 to September 1980, 421,854 people, or two per cent of the population, moved from one province to another province.

The rights outlined in these sections spell out the basic legal protection that will safeguard us in our dealings with the state and its machinery of justice. They are designed to protect the individual and to ensure simple fairness should he or she be subjected to legal proceedings, particularly criminal cases.

**8. Everyone has the right to be secure against
unreasonable search or seizure.**

**9. Everyone has the right not to be arbitrarily detained
or imprisoned.**

10. Everyone has the right on arrest or detention
  (*a*) to be informed promptly of the reasons therefor;
  **(*b*) to retain and instruct counsel without delay and
  to be informed of that right; and**
  **(*c*) to have the validity of the detention determined by
  way of *habeas corpus* and to be released if the
  detention is not lawful.**

*"Our society is anchored as well on openness of our
courts, and of our Legislative Assemblies, underpinned by
a universal franchise, on fair procedure before adjudica-
tive agencies, be they courts or other tribunals which, at
least, means a right to be heard or to make representa-
tions before being condemned criminally or made liable
civilly. In the administration of our criminal laws, special
protections have developed for an accused, such as the
rule against forced confessions, the presumption of innocence, and the privilege against self-incrimination. These
values are not absolutes, but a heavy burden lies on any
Legislative Assembly or Court to justify any attenuation
of these. The Canadian Bill of Rights, operative on the
federal level, has given sanctity to these values, short of
constitutional entrenchment."*

*The Right Honourable Chief Justice Bora Laskin, University of
Alberta, May 4, 1972*

11. Any person charged with an offence has the right
  **(*a*) to be informed without unreasonable delay of the
  specific offence;**
  (*b*) to be tried within a reasonable time;

These legal rights are an expansion of those included in the *Canadian Bill of Rights* of 1960, and most of them already exist in Canada by precedent and practice, or ordinary statute law. Enshrining them in the Constitution will ensure Canadians that they will not be able to be taken away from us easily by the state or its law enforcement agencies.

Specifically, we are guaranteed that the right to life, liberty and security of the individual will not be able to be taken away from us by the authorities of the state, except by laws and procedures that are lawful and fair.

These legal rights also prohibit unreasonable search or seizure. In addition, even though the law authorizing the search or seizure may be reasonable in itself, the manner in which it is executed by the police might be challenged as unreasonable in the circumstances; for instance, the police will not be able to use unnecessary force.

There is also the assurance that no person may be detained or held in an arbitrary manner. A police officer will have to show reasonable cause for detaining a person.

The rights on arrest or detention are designed to protect you against arbitrary or unlawful actions by law enforcement agencies. Therefore, anyone held or arrested by any authority will have the right to be told the reasons for being taken into custody, the right to be informed of the right to contact and consult a lawyer forthwith to obtain legal advice, and the right to have a court determine quickly whether the detention is lawful.

This section sets forth other important protections for any person charged with offences under federal or provincial law.

First, an accused person will have to be told promptly of the offence with which he or she has been charged, and brought to trial without undue delay. Also, the accused

(*c*) not to be compelled to be a witness in proceedings against that person in respect of the offence;
(*d*) to be presumed innocent until proven guilty according to law in a fair and public hearing by an independent and impartial tribunal;
(*e*) not to be denied reasonable bail without just cause;
(*f*) except in the case of an offence under military law tried before a military tribunal, to the benefit of trial by jury where the maximum punishment for the offence is imprisonment for five years or a more severe punishment;
(*g*) not to be found guilty on account of any act or omission unless, at the time of the act or omission, it constituted an offence under Canadian or international law or was criminal according to the general principles of law recognized by the community of nations;
(*h*) if finally acquitted of the offence, not to be tried for it again and, if finally found guilty and punished for the offence, not to be tried or punished for it again; and
(*i*) if found guilty of the offence and if the punishment for the offence has been varied between the time of commission and the time of sentencing, to the benefit of the lesser punishment.

Treatment or punishment

12. Everyone has the right not to be subjected to any cruel and unusual treatment or punishment.

Self-crimination

13. A witness who testifies in any proceedings has the right not to have any incriminating evidence so given used to incriminate that witness in any other proceedings, except in a prosecution for perjury or for the giving of contradictory evidence.

Interpreter

14. A party or witness in any proceedings who does not understand or speak the language in which the proceedings are conducted or who is deaf has the right to the assistance of an interpreter.

will not be able to be forced to take the stand at his or her own trial. In addition, a person will be entitled to be allowed reasonable bail.

Also under this section, everyone charged with an offence will have the right to be presumed innocent until proven guilty, and the right to trial by jury for serious charges.

Another provision makes it clear that a person cannot be convicted of an act or omission unless that act or omission is defined as an offence under Canadian or international law at the time the act or omission occurs. This will prevent the state from creating offences retroactively.

If a person should be tried and acquitted, he or she will not be able to be tried on the same charge again, or if found guilty and punished, will not be able to be tried or punished for it again.

And finally, take the hypothetical example of a new law that increases the fine or term of imprisonment for a given offence. If the crime is committed before the tougher penalties come into effect, but trial and conviction come afterward, the lesser penalty will apply.

Legal rights will ensure that no one is subjected to cruel and unusual punishment; that any witness will have an automatic right not to have incriminating evidence resulting from that testimony used against him or her in subsequent proceedings, except in special cases such as perjury; and, finally, that a party or witness in any proceedings, civil or criminal, will have the right to the assistance of an interpreter if he or she does not understand or speak the language of the proceedings or is deaf. This right will exist regardless of the language involved.

At the request of the Canadian Bar Association, Section 13 was amended to make it clear that the protection against self-incrimination will apply to a voluntary witness as well as to one who is compelled to testify.

Equality Rights

Equality before
and under law
and equal
protection and
benefit of law

15. (1) Every individual is equal before and under the law and has the right to the equal protection and equal benefit of the law without discrimination and, in particular, without discrimination based on race, national or ethnic origin, colour, religion, sex, age or mental or physical disability.

Affirmative
action programs

(2) Subsection (1) does not preclude any law, program or activity that has as its object the amelioration of conditions of disadvantaged individuals or groups including those that are disadvantaged because of race, national or ethnic origin, colour, religion, sex, age or mental or physical disability.

"We have the occasion . . . to build for our children and the children of our children a better Canada—a Canada which will recognize the diversity and equality which should be in our society, a Canada which will protect the weakest in society . . . a Canada which will be an example to the world."

The Honourable Jean Chrétien, House of Commons, February 17, 1981

". . . I would like this resolution, particularly the Charter of Rights and Freedoms, to hang on the wall of every classroom in every school in every region of Canada. I do not say this because I believe in propaganda. I say it because I believe constitutions are fundamentally about rights, rights are fundamentally about people and people from childhood on must be encouraged to acquire a deep understanding of their own liberties as well as an even deeper appreciation of the liberties of others."

Mr. Edward Broadbent, leader of the New Democratic Party, in the House of Commons, November 20, 1981

The equality rights included in the Charter will complement and add to the anti-discrimination provisions found in federal and provincial human rights legislation. This provision of the Charter comes into effect three years after patriation.

Under the Constitution all Canadians – regardless of race, national or ethnic origin, color, sex or age, as well as those who are physically or mentally disabled – will be equal before the law, and will enjoy equal protection and benefit of the law.

For the first time in Canadian history, the Constitution will make it clear that, for women, equality is not a right to be acquired, but a state that exists. It will ensure that women are entitled to full equality in law – and not just in the laws themselves but in the administration of law as well.

However, at the same time, nothing will rule out "affirmative action" programs designed to promote such things as equal employment opportunities for women.

Being handicapped is obviously a condition that requires special kinds of assistance and protection from discrimination. The Charter will, therefore, specifically allow for the establishment of special programs designed to promote opportunities for the disabled and will make certain these kinds of programs will be upheld by Canadian law.

Similarly, the Charter will also authorize affirmative action programs designed to improve the lot of other disadvantaged groups or individuals who may have suffered as a result of past discrimination.

Finally, the list of grounds of non-discrimination and the list for affirmative action is not exhaustive. This will enable the courts to develop new grounds of non-discrimination where the distinctions drawn are

Official Languages of Canada

Official
languages
of Canada

16. (1) English and French are the official languages of Canada and have equality of status and equal rights and privileges as to their use in all institutions of the Parliament and government of Canada.

Official
languages of
New Brunswick

(2) English and French are the official languages of New Brunswick and have equality of status and equal rights and privileges as to their use in all institutions of the legislature and government of New Brunswick.

Advancement of
status and use

(3) Nothing in this Charter limits the authority of Parliament or a legislature to advance the equality of status or use of English and French.

Proceedings
of Parliament

17. (1) Everyone has the right to use English or French in any debates and other proceedings of Parliament.

Proceedings of
New Brunswick
legislature

(2) Everyone has the right to use English or French in any debates and other proceedings of the legislature of New Brunswick.

Parliamentary
statutes and
records

18. (1) The statutes, records and journals of Parliament shall be printed and published in English and French and both language versions are equally authoritative.

New Brunswick
statutes and
records

(2) The statutes, records and journals of the legislature of New Brunswick shall be printed and published in English and French and both language versions are equally authoritative.

Proceedings in
courts established
by Parliament

19. (1) Either English or French may be used by any person in, or in any pleading in or process issuing from, any court established by Parliament.

considered unacceptable. This will also permit the development of affirmative action programs for other groups of people who may have suffered as a result of past discriminatory laws or practices.

The Charter confirms that English and French are Canada's official languages, meaning that you have the right, among other things, to communicate in English or French with the federal government and to receive services in the official language of your choice wherever there is a significant demand for services in that language. You also have the right to use English or French in Parliament and in all courts of law under federal jurisdiction. However, there is nothing in these sections that will require any member of the public to become bilingual. Rather, they will ensure that the federal government can serve members of the public in the official language of their choice.

The Charter also recognizes English and French as the official languages of New Brunswick, at the specific request of that province. The people of New Brunswick will have the constitutional right to use either official language in dealings with their government, in their legislative assembly and before the provincial courts. People of Quebec and Manitoba will continue to have the right to use either French or English in the provincial legislatures and before the courts of those provinces. The rights in these two provinces were established by the *BNA Act, 1867*, and the *Manitoba Act* of 1870.

(2) Either English or French may be used by any person in, or in any pleading in or process issuing from, any court of New Brunswick.

20. (1) Any member of the public in Canada has the right to communicate with, and to receive available services from, any head or central office of an institution of the Parliament or government of Canada in English or French, and has the same right with respect to any other office of any such institution where

(*a*) there is a significant demand for communications with and services from that office in such language; or

(*b*) due to the nature of the office, it is reasonable that communications with and services from that office be available in both English and French.

(2) Any member of the public in New Brunswick has the right to communicate with, and to receive available services from, any office of an institution of the legislature or government of New Brunswick in English or French.

21. Nothing in sections 16 to 20 abrogates or derogates from any right, privilege or obligation with respect to the English and French languages, or either of them, that exists or is continued by virtue of any other provision of the Constitution of Canada.

22. Nothing in sections 16 to 20 abrogates or derogates from any legal or customary right or privilege acquired or enjoyed either before or after the coming into force of this Charter with respect to any language that is not English or French.

"The proposed Charter also protects the use of the French and English languages. I agree that a new Constitution should preserve the existing constitutional rights and obligations respecting the French and English languages."

Honourable J. Angus MacLean, Premier of Prince Edward Island, before the Special Joint Committee, Ottawa, November 27, 1980

"The people who speak French in this country are not minorities. That is what the Official Languages Act says and that is what I want the Constitution to say. They are Canadians who exercise a right to speak one of the Canadian languages."

Honourable Richard Hatfield, Premier of New Brunswick, before the Special Joint Committee, Ottawa, December 4, 1980

"I do not object to the constitutional entrenchment of French and English language rights. The right to use French or English, or the right to receive some government services in either of those languages, is not, after all, a right which we claim as humans. It is an essential fact of Canada, an essential element of the Confederation bargain, and, as such, is an obvious candidate for inclusion in the Constitution."

Honourable Allan Blakeney, Premier of Saskatchewan, brief to the Special Joint Committee, Ottawa, December 19, 1980

Minority Language Educational Rights

Language of instruction

23. (1) Citizens of Canada
(*a*) whose first language learned and still understood is that of the English or French linguistic minority population of the province in which they reside, or
(*b*) who have received their primary school instruction in Canada in English or French and reside in a province where the language in which they received that instruction is the language of the English or French linguistic minority population of the province,

have the right to have their children receive primary and secondary school instruction in that language in that province.

21

This section of the Charter contains significant guarantees of minority language educational rights.

There are three main criteria that determine the rights of Canadian citizens of the English and French-speaking minorities in each province to have their children educated in their own language.

1. *Mother tongue.* If your mother tongue (first language learned and still understood) is French and you live in a mainly English-speaking province, you will have a constitutional right to have your children educated in French. This criterion is of vital importance to French-speaking Canadians outside Quebec as it ensures that

(2) Citizens of Canada of whom any child has received or is receiving primary or secondary school instruction in English or French in Canada, have the right to have all their children receive primary and secondary school instruction in the same language.

(3) The right of citizens of Canada under subsections (1) and (2) to have their children receive primary and secondary school instruction in the language of the English or French linguistic minority population of a province

(*a*) applies wherever in the province the number of children of citizens who have such a right is sufficient to warrant the provision to them out of public funds of minority language instruction; and

(*b*) includes, where the number of those children so warrants, the right to have them receive that instruction in minority language educational facilities provided out of public funds.

59. (1) Paragraph 23(1)(*a*) shall come into force in respect of Quebec on a day to be fixed by proclamation issued by the Queen or the Governor General under the Great Seal of Canada.

(2) A proclamation under subsection (1) shall be issued only where authorized by the legislative assembly or government of Quebec.

(3) This section may be repealed on the day paragraph 23(1)(*a*) comes into force in respect of Quebec and this Act amended and renumbered, consequential upon the repeal of this section, by proclamation issued by the Queen or the Governor General under the Great Seal of Canada.*

---

* Section 59 of the *Constitution Act*, 1982, is not a part of the Charter of Rights and Freedoms. However, it is reproduced here because it directly relates to the subject of minority language education rights.

French Canadian children have access to an education in French, even if their parents did not receive instruction in French.

2. *Language in which the parents were educated in Canada.* If you were educated in English in Canada and you live in Quebec, you can send your children to school in English in that province. Similarly, if you were educated in French in Canada and live in one of the other nine provinces, you can have your children educated in French in those provinces.

3. *Language in which other children in the family are receiving or have received their education.* If you have one child who has received primary or secondary school instruction in English or French in Canada, you have the right to have all your children educated in the same language.

All three criteria depend on there being enough children eligible for minority language education in an area to warrant setting up schools in that language for them out of public funds.

The second and third criteria – language in which parents and other children were educated – apply with respect to the minority language education systems (either French or English) in all 10 provinces. If you meet either of these criteria you are constitutionally guaranteed access to minority language education systems across Canada.

The first criterion – access by virtue of mother tongue – applies in all provinces except Quebec.

In order to accommodate Quebec's concerns, the constitutional resolution varies the application of the mother tongue criterion (Section 23(1) (a) of the *Constitution Act, 1982*) for Quebec. This criterion will not apply to Quebec unless and until authorized by the legislative assembly or government of Quebec.

"I think we agree with the idea that we must have a Charter of Rights in the Constitution, it is something that we have suggested for a long time; and finally, I think that the question of linguistic rights, Mr. Trudeau's idea to guarantee minority language educational rights across Canada, is something that we must do and do fast. Mr. Trudeau has worked for these rights courageously for 15 years now and as you know, we are in complete agreement. In effect, there is much that is good in this text."

Mr. Robert Bourassa, former premier of Quebec, Radio-Québec, November 2, 1980

Enforcement

Enforcement of guaranteed rights and freedoms

24. (1) Anyone whose rights or freedoms, as guaranteed by this Charter, have been infringed or denied may apply to a court of competent jurisdiction to obtain such remedy as the court considers appropriate and just in the circumstances.

Exclusion of evidence bringing administration of justice into disrepute

(2) Where, in proceedings under subsection (1), a court concludes that evidence was obtained in a manner that infringed or denied any rights or freedoms guaranteed by this Charter, the evidence shall be excluded if it is established that, having regard to all the circumstances, the admission of it in the proceedings would bring the administration of justice into disrepute.

Until that authorization is received, only citizens who
have been educated in English in Canada or have children educated in English in Canada have a constitutional right to have all their children educated in English in
Quebec.

This section of the Charter allows a person or groups
whose rights have been denied or infringed upon by law
or by action taken by the state to apply to a court for a
remedy deemed appropriate and just in the circumstances.

To illustrate how the enforcement provision might work,
consider the following examples. If some public servant
should attempt to prevent your group from religious
worship, you would be able to apply for a restraining
order and sue for damages, if any. If you were an
accused person and denied bail without just cause, you
would be able to apply to another court for a bail order.
If the police were to break into and search your premises
illegally and find evidence of a crime, the courts could
exclude such evidence in a subsequent trial in which it is
alleged that a right under the Charter has been
infringed, and if the Court finds that the admission of
such evidence would bring the administration of justice
into disrepute. This power to exclude evidence in limited
circumstances will permit the courts to preserve public
respect for the integrity of the judicial process.

General

25. The guarantee in this Charter of certain rights and freedoms shall not be construed so as to abrogate or derogate from any aboriginal, treaty or other rights or freedoms that pertain to the aboriginal peoples of Canada including

(*a*) any rights or freedoms that have been recognized by the Royal Proclamation of October 7, 1763; and
(*b*) any rights or freedoms that may be acquired by the aboriginal peoples of Canada by way of land claims settlement.

26. The guarantee in this Charter of certain rights and freedoms shall not be construed as denying the existence of any other rights or freedoms that exist in Canada.

There are a number of provisions in the Canadian Charter of Rights and Freedoms and elsewhere in the new Constitution that will recognize and affirm the rights of the native peoples of Canada – Indian, Inuit and Métis.

Special provisions were written into the Constitution at the request of native organizations. Representatives of these groups argued forcefully for recognition that would help their people preserve their culture and identity, their customs, traditions and languages.

Section 25 of the Charter makes it clear that no other provision can be used in a way that will interfere with any special rights that the native people have now or may acquire. For example, any new benefits they may gain from a settlement of land claims would not run afoul of the general equality rights as set out in the Charter.

Further on in the Constitution, Section 35 states that the existing aboriginal and treaty rights of the aboriginal peoples of Canada are recognized and affirmed.

Moreover, there is a written commitment that within one year after the Constitution comes into force the Prime Minister will convene a constitutional conference that will include in its agenda an item respecting the aboriginal peoples of Canada. Representatives of the native peoples will be invited to participate in the conference.

This section ensures that, by specifically guaranteeing certain rights and freedoms in the Charter, the existence of any other rights will not be denied. In other words, the Charter does not pretend to be an exhaustive document concerning the rights of Canadians. What it does do is entrench *minimum* rights. Nothing in the Charter will be able to prevent Parliament or legislatures from adding to our rights.

**27. This Charter shall be interpreted in a manner
consistent with the preservation and enhancement of the
multicultural heritage of Canadians.**

*"In (the new) Parliament there will be no question of race,
nationality, religion or locality . . . The basis of action
adopted by the delegates to the Quebec Conference in
preparing the resolutions was to do justice to all – justice
to all races, to all religions, to all nationalities and to all
interests . . ."*

Sir Hector-Louis Langevin, Father of Confederation, 1865

*"For here (in Canada), I want the marble to remain the
marble; the granite to remain the granite; the oak to
remain the oak; and out of all of these elements, I would
build a nation great among the nations of the world."*

Prime Minister Sir Wilfrid Laurier, 1903

*"Canada is a garden . . . into which has been transplanted
the hardiest and brightest flowers of many lands, each
retaining in its new environment the best of the qualities
for which it was loved and prized in its native lands . . ."*

The Right Honourable John G. Diefenbaker, 1961

**28. Notwithstanding anything in this Charter, the rights
and freedoms referred to in it are guaranteed equally to
male and female persons.**

Canadians are proud that this country has not become a melting pot, but has maintained its multicultural character. This is officially recognized in the Constitution under the provisions of the Charter stating that it shall be interpreted in such a way as to maintain and enhance the multicultural heritage of Canada.

This special clause ensures that all rights in the Charter are guaranteed equally to men and women. It was added at the request of women's groups to provide reassurance that their rights will be protected. This is one guarantee that *cannot* be overriden by a legislature or Parliament.

Rights
respecting
certain schools
preserved

29. Nothing in this Charter abrogates or derogates from any rights or privileges guaranteed by or under the Constitution of Canada in respect of denominational, separate or dissentient schools.

Application to
territories and
territorial
authorities

30. A reference in this Charter to a province or to the legislative assembly or legislature of a province shall be deemed to include a reference to the Yukon Territory and the Northwest Territories, or to the appropriate legislative authority thereof, as the case may be.

Legislative
powers not
extended

31. Nothing in this Charter extends the legislative powers of any body or authority.

The establishment and operation of religious schools will not be adversely affected by any other provisions of the Charter.

This ensures, for example, that neither the freedom of conscience and religion clause nor the equality rights clause, will be interpreted so as to strike down existing constitutional rights respecting the establishment and state financing of schools operated on a religious basis, with students and teachers selected according to their adherence to a particular religious faith.

This provision makes it clear that the Charter applies equally to the Yukon Territory and the Northwest Territories as it does to the provinces.

This section simply states the basic rule that nothing in the Charter will be intended to affect the distribution of powers carried over from the *British North America Act* as between Parliament and the provincial legislatures. The Charter neither transfers powers from the provincial to the federal order nor vice versa. What it does is ensure that Canadians will enjoy their basic rights without undue restraint by either order of government.

The Charter defines the relationship between government and citizens with respect to their rights and freedoms. Protection of rights as between individuals will continue to be governed by federal and provincial human rights laws.

Application of Charter

32. (1) This Charter applies

(*a*) to the Parliament and government of Canada in respect of all matters within the authority of Parliament including all matters relating to the Yukon Territory and Northwest Territories; and

(*b*) to the legislature and government of each province in respect of all matters within the authority of the legislature of each province.

(2) Notwithstanding subsection (1), section 15 shall not have effect until three years after this section comes into force.

33. (1) Parliament or the legislature of a province may expressly declare in an Act of Parliament or of the legislature, as the case may be, that the Act or a provision thereof shall operate nothwithstanding a provision included in section 2 or sections 7 to 15 of this Charter.

(2) An Act or a provision of an Act in respect of which a declaration made under this section is in effect shall have such operation as it would have but for the provision of this Charter referred to in the declaration.

(3) A declaration made under subsection (1) shall cease to have effect five years after it comes into force or on such earlier date as may be specified in the declaration.

(4) Parliament or a legislature of a province may re-enact a declaration made under subsection (1).

(5) Subsection (3) applies in respect of a re-enactment made under subsection (4).

Except for section 15, dealing with equality rights, which will come into effect three years after actual patriation, all the other sections of the Charter apply at the time of patriation throughout Canada at the federal, provincial and territorial levels.

The reason for delay in applying the equality provisions is to give the federal, provincial and territorial governments time to review and change any laws that may not conform to the safeguards that will be provided by that section. This will eliminate a considerable amount of unnecessary and expensive legal action.

Under the agreement that broke the constitutional deadlock, both Parliament and provincial legislatures will retain a limited power to pass laws that may conflict with parts of the Charter of Rights concerning fundamental freedoms, legal rights and equality rights.

However, in order to do so, Parliament or a legislature will have to insert a clause declaring specifically that it is passing the law *notwithstanding* specified provisions of the Charter of Rights.

In addition, any federal or provincial law containing a "notwithstanding," or override clause, will have to be reviewed and the declaration re-enacted at least every five years or it will not remain in force.

In other words, if a government should propose a law that may limit some of the rights and freedoms set out in the Charter, it will have to say clearly that this is what it is doing and accept full responsibility for the political consequences.

"It (the legislative override) might actually encourage the courts to be more imaginative than they have been thus far. This has been one of the fears of the people who are opposed to the Bill of Rights, and that is that our court record thus far on the existing Bill of Rights wasn't that good. It's possible that what you now have arranged for in the protection of civil liberties would be an interplay between courts and Parliament. In other words, you won't be able to take away human rights without making it patent that you're doing so, and at the same stage the courts might say a certain law contravenes the Charter. It will make that whole argument public."

Mr. Walter Tarnopolsky, former president of the Canadian Civil Liberties Association, in an interview on Sunday Morning, CBC Radio Network, November 8, 1981

"The 'notwithstanding' clauses will be a red flag for opposition parties and the press ... That will make it politically difficult for a government to override the Charter. Political difficulty is a reasonable safeguard for the Charter."

"Canada at the moment is a parliamentary democracy in which the will of Parliament is supreme. If there were no notwithstandings in the proposed Constitution, this supremacy would shift to the judges who would decide whether or not a law offended the Constitution."

"By making it legally possible but politically difficult to override the Charter, they have married the two notions ... The result is a strong Charter with an escape valve for the legislatures."

Canadian Press news item, quoting Mr. Alan Borovoy, legal council to the Canadian Civil Liberties Association, in the Calgary Herald, Nov. 7, 1981

It is important to note that an override clause is very different from an "opting out" provision. No province will be able to opt out of the Charter of Rights and Freedoms.

Furthermore, as was noted earlier in this publication, the override clause will ensure that legislatures rather than judges have the final say on important matters of public policy, and that the Charter will continue to reflect our changing social values.

There is nothing new about the concept of an override clause. Similar clauses appear in the *Alberta Bill of Rights*, the *Saskatchewan Human Rights Code*, the *Quebec Charter of Rights and Freedoms,* and the *Canadian Bill of Rights*.

Citation

Citation

34. This Part may be cited as the *Canadian Charter of Rights and Freedoms.*

"The adoption of a Charter of Rights would be a public act enabling us to realize the dream we have nurtured of freedom and equality before the law everywhere across Canada."

Mr. Claude Ryan, leader of the Quebec Liberal Party, National Press Club, Ottawa, December 12, 1980

This section simply provides that the Charter shall be known as the Canadian Charter of Rights and Freedoms.

Should you wish to obtain more information about your rights, you may, as a first recourse, contact your federal Member of Parliament, your Member of the provincial Legislative Assembly or any of the following federal agencies for guidance.

For information on equality rights:

Canadian Human Rights Commission

National Office

Canadian Human Rights
Commission
257 Slater Street
Ottawa, Ontario
K1A 1E1

Ontario Region

Arthur Meighen Building
Room 623
55 St. Clair Avenue East
Toronto, Ontario
M4T 1M2

Atlantic Region

Office address:
Lord Nelson Arcade
Room 212
5675 Spring Garden Road
Halifax, Nova Scotia
B3J 1H1

Mailing address:
P.O. Box 3545
Halifax South Postal Station
Halifax, Nova Scotia
B3J 3J2

Prairie Region

Kensington Building
Room 1804
275 Portage Avenue
Winnipeg, Manitoba
R3B 2B3

Alberta and Northwest Territories Region

Liberty Building
Room 416
10506 Jasper Avenue
Edmonton, Alberta
T5J 2W9

Quebec Region

Room 1115
2021 Union Avenue
Montreal, Quebec
H3A 2S9

Western Region

Montreal Trust Building
Room 1002, 789 West Pender
Vancouver, British Columbia
V6C 1H2

For information on the rights of women:

Canadian Advisory Council on the Status of Women

18th Floor
66 Slater Street
P.O. Box 1541, Station B
Ottawa, Canada
K1P 5R5

Room 205
666 Sherbrooke Street West
Montreal, Quebec
H3A 1E7

Room 600
269 Main Street
Winnipeg, Manitoba
R3C 1B2

P.O. Box 5174
Vancouver, British Columbia
V6B 4B2

For information on official language rights:

Commissioner of Official Languages

National Office

66 Slater Street
Ottawa, Canada
K1A 0T8

Manitoba, Saskatchewan
and Northwestern Ontario

P.O. Box 96
Norwood Grove
Winnipeg, Manitoba
R2H 3B8

Alberta, British Columbia,
Yukon and Northwest Territories

11th Floor
Liberty Building
10506 Jasper Avenue
Edmonton, Alberta
T5J 2W9

Central and Western Ontario

6th Floor
127 Cedar Street
Sudbury, Ontario
P3E 1B1

Quebec

6th Floor
615 Dorchester Boulevard West
Montreal, Quebec
H3B 1P5

Atlantic Provinces

P.O. Box 1125
Moncton, New Brunswick
E1C 8P6

For information concerning official languages in the
federal public service, including language of work and
service to the public:

Official Languages Branch
Treasury Board Secretariat
Vanier Building
222 Nepean Street
Ottawa, Canada
K1A 0R5

Appendix A

Groups and individuals who appeared and gave evidence before the Special Joint Committee of the Senate and the House of Commons on the Constitution (listed in alphabetical order)

Advisory Council on the Status of Women
Afro-Asian Foundation of Canada
Aird, P. L. Professor, Faculty of Forestry, University of
    Toronto
Alberta Chamber of Commerce
Alberta Social Credit Party
Algonquin Council
Alliance for Life
Association canadienne-française de l'Ontario
Association culturelle franco-canadienne de la
    Saskatchewan
Association of Iroquois and Allied Indians
Association of Métis and Non-Status Indians of Saskatchewan
Attikamek-Montagnais Council

British Columbia Civil Liberties Association
Business Council on National Issues

Campaign Life Canada
Canada West Foundation
Canadian Abortion Rights Action League
Canadian Association for the Prevention of Crime
Canadian Association of Chiefs of Police
Canadian Association of Crown Counsels
Canadian Association of Lesbians and Gay Men
Canadian Association for the Mentally Retarded
Canadian Association of Social Workers
Canadian Bar Association
Canadian Bar Association, Newfoundland Branch
Canadian Catholic School Trustees' Association
Canadian Chamber of Commerce
Canadian Citizenship Federation
Canadian Civil Liberties Association
Canadian Committee on Learning Opportunities for Women
Canadian Conference of Catholic Bishops
Canadian Connection
Canadian Consultative Council on Multiculturalism
Canadian Council on Children and Youth
Canadian Council on Social Development
Canadian Federation of Civil Liberties and Human Rights
    Associations
Canadians for Canada
Canadians for One Canada
Canadian Human Rights Commission
Canadian Jewish Congress

Canadian Life Insurance Association
Canadian National Institute for the Blind
Canadian Polish Congress
Chrétien, Jean (The Honourable), Minister of Justice and
    Attorney General of Canada
Church of Jesus Christ of Latter Day Saints
Coalition for the Protection of Human Life
Coalition of Provincial Organizations of the Handicapped
Council for Yukon Indians
Council of National Ethnocultural Organizations of Canada
Council of Quebec Minorities

Denominational Educational Committees of Newfoundland
Department of Justice

la Fédération des francophones hors Québec
Federation of Canadian Municipalities
Federation of Independent Schools of Canada
Federation of Saskatchewan Indians

German-Canadian Committee on the Constitution
Government of New Brunswick
Government of Nova Scotia
Government of Prince Edward Island
Government of Saskatchewan
Government of the Northwest Territories
Government of the Yukon Territory

Indian Association of Alberta
Indian Rights for Indian Women
Inuit Committee on National Issues
Italian-Canadians National Congress (Quebec Region)

Love, Dean D. V.

Media Club of Canada
Mennonite Central Committee (Canada)

National Action Committee on the Status of Women
National Anti-Poverty Organizations
National Association of Japanese Canadians
National Association of Women and the Law
National Black Coalition of Canada
National Indian Brotherhood
Native Council of Canada
Native Women's Association of Canada
New Brunswick Human Rights Commission
New Democratic Party of Alberta
Nishga Tribal Council
Nuu-Chah-Nulth Tribal Council

Ontario Conference of Catholic Bishops

Parti de l'Union nationale du Québec
People's Law School Society and Social Planning and Review
    Council of British Columbia

Positive Action Committee
Progressive Conservative Party of Saskatchewan
Protestant School Board of Greater Montreal
Public Interest Advocacy Centre

Russell, Professor Peter H.

Saskatchewan Human Rights Commission
la Société Franco-manitobaine

Ukrainian Canadian Committee
Union of New Brunswick Indians
Union of Nova Scotia Indians
Union of Ontario Indians
United Church of Canada

Vancouver People's Law School Society

World Federalists of Canada – Operation Dismantle

Yalden, M. F., Commissioner of Official Languages

Appendix B

List of groups and individuals whose written submissions
were received by the Special Joint Committee of the
Senate and the House of Commons, on or before
February 2, 1981

A
Abbass, Cyril J. – Willowdale, Ontario
Adams, Grethyll – Prince Albert, Saskatchewan
Adams, Helen – Collingwood, Ontario
Addington, Charles – London, Ontario
Adler, Simon – Kitchener, Ontario
Advisory Council on the Status of Women – Ottawa, Ontario
Affiliation of Multicultural Societies of British
    Columbia – Kamloops, British Columbia
Afro-Asian Foundation of Canada – Montreal, Quebec
Agarwal, S. C. – Mississauga, Ontario
Agudath, Israël – Toronto, Ontario
Aird, Deborah – London, Ontario

Aird, Paul L. – Toronto, Ontario
Albert, J. M. – Vancouver, B.C.
Alberta Chamber of Commerce – Edmonton, Alberta
Alberta Committee of Action Groups of the Disabled –
    Calgary, Alberta
Alberta Lesbian and Gay Rights Association – Edmonton,
    Alberta
Alberta Liberal Party – Calgary, Alberta
Alberta New Democratic Party – Edmonton, Alberta
Alberta Public Policy Committee – Edmonton, Alberta
Alberta Real Estate Association – Calgary, Alberta
Alberta Status of Women Action Committee – Edmonton,
    Alberta
Alberta Women for Constitution Change – Calgary, Alberta
Albo, Carol – Rossland, British Columbia
Alcock, Stuart – Vancouver, British Columbia
Aldwinckle, Mary C. – Ottawa, Ontario
Algonquin Council – Val d'Or, Quebec
Allen, H. – Ouathiaski Cove, British Columbia
Alliance for Life – Winnipeg, Manitoba
Allier, Irène – Montreal, Quebec
Allison, E. F. – Calgary, Alberta
Allistone, Ernie F. – Vancouver, British Columbia
Amdur, Reuel S. – Toronto, Ontario
Amys, John Hewitt – Toronto, Ontario
Anderson, Bruce W. – Fredericton, New Brunswick
Anderson Lake Band – D'Arcy, British Columbia
Andrews, Ralph – Edmonton, Alberta
Anglican Church of Canada – Toronto, Ontario
Anglican Church of Canada – London, Ontario
Angus, J. F. – Calgary, Alberta
Ardito, Ann
Ardito, Dorothy
Ardito, John E.
Ardito, Mary
Ardito, Paul J.
Ardito, Paul M.
Archer, R. Douglas – Vancouver, British Columbia
Armitage, D. P. – Brampton, Ontario
Armstrong, Ralph C. – Edmonton, Alberta
Assad, Jocelyne
Asselstine, Asta – Winnipeg, Manitoba
Assemblée nationale du Québec – Quebec, Quebec
Associated Disabled Persons of B.C. – Victoria,
    British Columbia
Association of Catholic Parents (English Section) of the Stor-
    mont, Dundas, Glengarry Board of Education – Ottawa,
    Ontario
Association of Canadian Clubs – Ottawa, Ontario
Association canadienne d'éducation de langue française
Association canadienne-française de l'Alberta – Edmonton,
    Alberta

Association canadienne-française de l'Ontario, Conseil
régional des Mille-Îles – Kingston, Ontario

ACFO – Windsor, Ontario

ACFO – Cornwall, Ontario

ACFO – Ottawa, Ontario

Association culturelle franco-canadienne de la Saskatchewan –
Regina, Saskatchewan

Association des francophones du Nord-Ouest de l'Ontario –
Thunder Bay, Ontario.

Association of Gay Social Service Workers – Toronto, Ontario

Association of Iroquois and Allied Indians – Wallaceburg,
Ontario

Association des juristes d'expression française de l'Ontario –
Ottawa, Ontario

Association of Métis and Non-Status Indians of Saskatchewan
– Regina, Saskatchewan

Association progressiste conservatrice fédérale du Québec –
Montreal, Quebec

Athabaska Chipewyan Band 201 – Fort Chipewyan, Alberta

Atkinson College Council – Downsview, Ontario

Atlantic Provinces Economic Council – Halifax, Nova Scotia

Attikamek Montagnais Council – Village des Hurons, Quebec

Aultman, Richard – Powassan, Ontario

Aultman, Ruth – Powassan, Ontario

Austin, G. H. – Calgary, Alberta

Austman, Linda – Calgary, Alberta

Awan, Sadig Noor Alan – Ottawa, Ontario

B

Baechler, F. E. – Powassan, Ontario

Baer, Ted J. – Calgary, Alberta

Baig, B. Lee – Thunder Bay, Ontario

Bailey, Walter S. – Toronto, Ontario

Baker, Bryan J. N. – Don Mills, Ontario

Baker, Norman – Regina, Saskatchewan

The Baltic Federation in Canada – Toronto, Ontario

Barabas, Joe – Guelph, Ontario

Barber-Starkey, Joe – Victoria, British Columbia

Barclay, Donald R. – Kitchener, Ontario

Barclay, Eric H. – Pickering, Ontario

Baril, Yves Réginald – Ottawa, Ontario

Barker, Harold W. – Scarborough, Ontario

Barman, Teresa – London, Ontario

Barrett, Bernice – Oshawa, Ontario

Barrett, Erica – North Vancouver, British Columbia

Barth, Joe – London, Ontario

Bartholomew, Michael – Ottawa, Ontario

Basavarajappa, K. G. – Nepean, Ontario

Basilian Fathers – Toronto, Ontario

Bawden, Edward – Montreal, Quebec

Bearcroft, Norma – Salmon Arm, British Columbia
Beaton, Floyd M. – Powassan, Ontario
Beaton, John W. (Mr. & Mrs.) – Ajax, Ontario
Beaudry, Diane – St. Thomas, Ontario
Beaujot, Roderic – London, Ontario
Beauvais, Jean-Claude & Lisette – Hull, Quebec
Beazley, Dorothy – Calgary, Alberta
Beckton, Clare F. – Halifax, Nova Scotia
Bédard, Daniel – Armstrong, British Columbia
Beecher Bay Band – Nanaimo, British Columbia
Beecher, Leo P. – Toronto, Ontario
Beesley, Ken B. – Vancouver, British Columbia
Beeston, H. C. – Downsview, Ontario
Beeston, Marion – Downsview, Ontario
Beke, A. John – Regina, Saskatchewan
Béland, André – Beauport, Quebec
Belfry, Rob – London, Ontario
Belkin, Elliott J. – Vancouver, British Columbia
Bell, Jim – Calgary, Alberta
Bell, Ronald G. – Peterborough, Ontario
Bennett, Ferne – Toronto, Ontario
Benson, Quennie & Robert – Toronto, Ontario
Benton, S. B. – Fredericton, New Brunswick
Bentz, Peter – Thunder Bay, Ontario
Berdan, Jack – Alvinston, Ontario
Berg, John H. – Calgary, Alberta
Berge, Anne & Lawrence – Pickering, Ontario
Bernard, H. H. – London, Ontario
Bernarz, John – Iroquois Falls, Ontario
Bertrand, Daniel – Dorval, Quebec
Bible Holiness Movement – Vancouver, British Columbia
Bickis, Mikelis G. – Ottawa, Ontario
Biggs, Evelyn V. – White Rock, British Columbia
Birch, G. S. – Calgary, Alberta
Bird, William E. – Belleville, Ontario
Black, William – Vancouver, British Columbia
Blakely, H. C. – Regina, Saskatchewan
Blind Organization of Ontario with Selfhelp Tactics –
   Toronto, Ontario
Blitstein, G. – Aldergrove, British Columbia
Blueberry Band – Blueberry Reserve, British Columbia
Board of Education for the City of Toronto – Toronto, Ontario
Bob, Wannita – Vedder Crossing, Manitoba
Bockmann, Walter – Toronto, Ontario
Boehm, Arnold H. – Ottawa, Ontario
Boehnke, Richard – Islington, Ontario
Boivin, Pierre – Quebec, Quebec
Bolwerk, Peter – Powassan, Ontario
Bordeleau, André G. – Guelph, Ontario
Borough of Etobicoke – Etobicoke, Ontario
Boucher, Ken – Mission, British Columbia
Boucher, Lillian – Ottawa, Ontario

Boucquez, Doug – Cobourg, Ontario
Bourget, Clément – Montreal, Quebec
Bouri, Mary
Bouri, Terry
Bowyer, Joseph – Windsor, Ontario
Boyle, Merrijane – St. Paul, New Brunswick
Boyle, Theresa M. – Mississauga, Ontario
Bradford, Art – Orillia, Ontario
Braunberger, H. A. – Orleans, Ontario
Brennan, J. – Islington, Ontario
Brewis, D. W. – Victoria, British Columbia
Briggs, Robert S. B. B. – Surrey, British Columbia
Brisbin, J. E. – Three Hills, Alberta
British Columbia Chamber of Commerce – Vancouver,
    British Columbia
British Columbia Civil Liberties Association – Vancouver,
    British Columbia
B.C. Federation of Labour – Burnaby, British Columbia
British Columbia Human Rights Symposium – Vernon,
    British Columbia
British Columbia Medical Association – Vancouver, British
    Columbia
British Columbia Provincial Council of Carpenters –
    Vancouver, British Columbia
Britton, Sid H. – Aurora, Ontario
Brock, Georgia – Port Perry, Ontario
Brooks, Kathleen – London, Ontario
Brooks, Lorne – Calgary, Alberta
Brooks, Phillip – Fort Saskatchewan, Alberta
Brooymans, Mary Ann – Port Stanley, Ontario
Brow, Betty – Vancouver, British Columbia
Brown, Anne J. – Calgary, Alberta
Brown, Helen R. – Saskatoon, Saskatchewan
Browne, G. P. – Ottawa, Ontario
Brunelle, Jacques M. – Sudbury, Ontario
Bruning, O. H. – Swift Current, Saskatchewan
Brunton, Richard – Ottawa, Ontario
Brunton, William – Simcoe, Ontario
Bryson, Peter M. – Halifax, Nova Scotia
Bubar, S. L. – Midway, British Columbia
Buck, Frank – Lantzville, British Columbia
Buck, Zena – Lantzville, British Columbia
Bufton, Audrey – Ottawa, Ontario
Burness, James N. – Lethbridge, Alberta
Burrard Indian Band – North Vancouver, British Columbia
Busby, William C. – Scarborough, Ontario
Business Council on National Issues – Toronto, Ontario
Bustard, Ernest E. – Oakville, Ontario
Butler, David E. – Calgary, Alberta
Buttery, J. W. L. – Galiano, British Columbia
Bydwell, Howard William – Kingston, Ontario

C

Cain, Sandy – Niagara Falls, Ontario
Caldwell, M. C. – Calgary, Alberta
Calgary Action Group of the Disabled – Calgary, Alberta
Calgary Chamber of Commerce – Calgary, Alberta
Calgary Civil Liberties Association – Calgary, Alberta
Camateros, Stylianos – Ste-Foy, Quebec
Cameron, Don – Kamloops, British Columbia
Cameron, Neil – Minnedosa, Manitoba
Cameron, Norma – Ottawa, Ontario
Campaign Life Canada – Edmonton, Alberta
Campbell, A. J. – Nepean, Ontario
Campbell, Dorothy J. – Halifax, Nova Scotia
Campbell, Jean D. – Toronto, Ontario
Campbell, Margaret – Vernon, British Columbia
Campbell, Maurice R. – Vancouver, British Columbia
Campbell, R. – Vernon, British Columbia
Camrose R. C. Separate School District No. 60 – Camrose,
    Alberta
Canada West Foundation – Calgary, Alberta
Canadian Abortion Rights Action League (CARAL)
    – Toronto, Ontario
Canadian Association of Chiefs of Police – Ottawa, Ontario
Canadian Association of Crown Counsels – Toronto, Ontario
Canadian Association of Lesbians and Gay Men – Ottawa,
    Ontario
Canadian Association for the Mentally Retarded –
    Downsview, Ontario
Canadian Association for the Prevention of Crime – Ottawa,
    Ontario
Canadian Association of Schools of Social Work – Ottawa,
    Ontario
Canadian Association of Social Workers – Ottawa, Ontario
Canadian Bar Association – Ottawa, Ontario
Canadian Bar Association – B.C. Branch
Canadian Bureau of the North American Jewish Students'
    Network – Toronto, Ontario
Canadian Catholic School Trustees Association – Toronto,
    Ontario
Canadian Cattle Consultants – Calgary, Alberta
Canadian Chamber of Commerce – Montreal, Quebec
Canadian Citizens Constitution Committee – Calgary, Alberta
Canadian Citizenship Federation – Ottawa, Ontario
Canadian Civil Liberties Association – Toronto, Ontario
Canadian Committee for the International Union for Conser-
    vation of Nature and Natural Resources – Ottawa, Ontario
Canadian Committee on Learning Opportunities for Women –
    Toronto, Ontario
Canadian Conference of the Arts – Ottawa, Ontario
Canadian Conference of Catholic Bishops – Ottawa, Ontario
Canadian Conference on Religion and World Peace – Toronto,
    Ontario

Canadian Congress for Learning Opportunities for Women –
Toronto, Ontario
Canadian Connection – Ottawa, Ontario
Canadian Consultative Council on Multiculturalism –
Edmonton, Alberta
Canadian Co-ordinating Council of Deafness – Ottawa,
Ontario
Canadian Copyright Institute – Toronto, Ontario
Canadian Council of the Blind – London, Ontario
Canadian Council on Children and Youth – Ottawa, Ontario
Canadian Council of Christians and Jews – Vancouver,
British Columbia
Canadian Council for Exceptional Children – Vancouver,
British Columbia
Canadian Council on Social Development – Ottawa, Ontario
Canadian Crafts Council – Ottawa, Ontario
Canadian Federation of Business and Professional Women's
Clubs – Ottawa, Ontario
Canadian Federation of Civil Liberties and Human Rights
Associations – Ottawa, Ontario
Canadian Federation of University Women – Toronto, Ontario
Canadian Health Coalition – Ottawa, Ontario
Canadian Forestry Association – Ottawa, Ontario
Canadian Home Economics Association – Ottawa, Ontario
Canadian Human Rights Commission – Ottawa, Ontario
Canadian Human Rights Foundation – Montreal, Quebec
Canadian Indian Lawyers' Association – Regina,
Saskatchewan
Canadian Jewish Congress – Montreal, Quebec
Canadian Labour Congress – Ottawa, Ontario
Canadian League of Rights – Flesherton, Ontario
Canadian Life Insurance Association – Toronto, Ontario
Canadian Mental Health Association – Toronto, Ontario
Canadian National Institute for the Blind – Toronto, Ontario
Canadian Organization of Small Business – Edmonton,
Alberta
Canadian Paraplegic Association – Toronto, Ontario
Canadian Parents for French – Ottawa, Ontario
Canadian Parents for French, Alberta Branch – Calgary,
Alberta
Canadian Physicians for Life – Hamilton, Ontario
Canadian Polish Congress – Toronto, Ontario
Canadian Protestant League – London, Ontario
Canadian Real Estate Association – Don Mills (Toronto),
Ontario
Canadian Rehabilitation Council for the Disabled – Toronto,
Ontario
Canadian Slovak League – Ottawa, Ontario
Canadian Society for Professional Engineers – Toronto,
Ontario
Canadian Sebobran – Hamilton, Ontario
Canadian Teachers' Federation – Ottawa, Ontario

Canadians for Canada – Grafton, Ontario
Canadians in Defence of Labour Rights – Toronto, Ontario
Canadians for One Canada – Winnipeg, Manitoba
Canadians for Responsible Government – Ottawa, Ontario
Canadians United for Separation of Church and State
    – Vancouver, British Columbia
Cape Breton Right to Life – Sydney, Nova Scotia
Carbonneau, Louis-Roy – Quebec, Quebec
Cardinal Léger Secondary School – Brampton, Ontario
Carmichael, Dolina A. – Edmonton, Alberta
Carrier, Jean – Thetford Mines, Quebec
Carroll, Joseph P. – Ajax, Ontario
Carruthers, Allan – Vancouver, British Columbia
Carruthers, Joanne – Cambridge, Ontario
Carson, William – Vancouver, British Columbia
Carson, Kathleen – Vancouver, British Columbia
Carson, Andrew R. – Vancouver, British Columbia
Caswell, Gay White – Saskatoon, Saskatchewan
Catholic Women's League of Canada – Winnipeg, Manitoba
Catholic Women's League of Canada, Sault Ste-Marie
    Regional Council – Sault Ste-Marie, Ontario
Celentano, Shirley – North Bay, Ontario
Centre for Continuing Education – Halifax, Nova Scotia
Chahley, William – Rothesay, New Brunswick
Chataway, Peter J. – Kelowna, British Columbia
Cheslatta Band – Cheslatta Indian Reserve, British Columbia
Cheston, Bruce & Linda – Regina, Saskatchewan
Chevaliers de Colomb, Conseil no 6881 – Clarence Creek,
    Ontario
Childs, Fred & Family – Calgary, Alberta
Chillingworth, N. Lorraine – Nepean, Ontario
Chinese Benevolent Association of Vancouver – Vancouver,
    British Columbia
Chinese-Canadian Council for Equality – Vancouver,
    British Columbia
Chipmen, H.R. – Halifax, Nova Scotia
Chippendale, Anne – Calgary, Alberta
Christian Labour Association of Canada – Rexdale, Ontario
Christian Reformed Church of Williamsburg – Williamsburg,
    Ontario
Christian Science Committee on Publication for Ontario –
    Toronto, Ontario
Christian Science Federal Representative for Canada
    – Toronto, Ontario
Christian, William – Guelph, Ontario
Church, Betty – Brampton, Ontario
Church of Jesus Christ of Latter Day Saints – Toronto,
    Ontario
Citizens' Advisory Council of the West Island of Montreal –
    Montreal, Quebec
Citizens Association to Save the Environment – Victoria,
    British Columbia

The Citizens for More Time Committee – Vernon,
  British Columbia
Clancy, Dorothy C. – Edmonton, Alberta
Clark, Keiron – Toronto, Ontario
Clark, Lynda-Anne – Ottawa, Ontario
Clarke, Alan – Ottawa, Ontario
Clarke, Anne – Victoria, British Columbia
Cleveland, George – McGrath, Alberta
Cloutier, Denys – Sherbrooke, Quebec
Cloutier, Edouard – Montreal, Quebec
Coalition for the Protection of Human Life – Toronto, Ontario
Coalition of Provincial Organizations of the Handicapped –
  Winnipeg, Manitoba
Coats, David – Ajax, Ontario
Coates, H. (Mr. & Mrs.) – Prince George, British Columbia
Codling, Doug (Pastor) – Richmond, British Columbia
Cohen, Maxwell – Ottawa, Ontario
Coldstream Friends Meeting – Ilderton, Ontario
Coldwater Indian Reserve – Merritt, British Columbia
Coley, V. H. – Edmonton, Alberta
Coll, Philip – Guelph, Ontario
Collie, Ronald A. – Calgary, Alberta
Collins, John E. – Calgary, Alberta
Collyer, Muriel – Leamington, Ontario
Colwill-Maddock, M. – Muskoka Lake, Ontario
Comité consultatif de langue française, comté de Simcoe
  – Penetanguishene, Ontario
Le Comité Culturel d'Oshawa – Oshawa, Ontario
Commission on Legislation and Civic Action of Agudath
  Israel of Canada – Toronto, Ontario
Commissioner of Official Languages – Ottawa, Ontario
Committee of the Council of Disabled (National Capital
  Region) – Ottawa, Ontario
Committee of Canadian Communists – Regina, Saskatchewan
Committee of Canadian Communists, Vancouver Branch –
  Vancouver, British Columbia
Committee for Constitutional Awareness – Mississauga,
  Ontario
Committee to Democratize the Constitutional Debate –
  Toronto, Ontario
Committee for Justice and Liberty Foundation – Toronto,
  Ontario
Committee for Racial Equality – Toronto, Ontario
Committee for Racial Justice – Vancouver, British Columbia
Communist Party of Canada – Toronto, Ontario
Community Business and Professional Association –
  Vancouver, British Columbia
Concerned Citizens of Toronto – Toronto, Ontario
Congress of Linguists – Winnipeg, Manitoba
Conklin, W.E. – Windsor, Ontario
Connely, Michael – Toronto, Ontario
51   Conroy, John W. – Mission, British Columbia

Conseil francophone de planification scolaire d'Ottawa-
 Carleton – Ottawa, Ontario
Conseil de la langue française du Québec – Quebec, Quebec
Conseil de vie française – Cornwall, Ontario
Conservation Council of Ontario – Toronto, Ontario
Conway, Terry J. – Windsor, Ontario
Cook, Ernest – Powassan, Ontario
Cook, Lillian – Powassan, Ontario
Cooke, Ellen – Winnipeg, Manitoba
Cooper, K. Eilleen – Calgary, Alberta
Corcoran, Catherine – Islington, Ontario
Corcoran, Don – Islington, Ontario
Corcoran, Marg – Islington, Ontario
Corcoran, Pat – Islington, Ontario
The Corporation of the Brothers of the Sacred Heart of
 Ontario – Ottawa, Ontario
Costly, Anne and family – Burnaby, British Columbia
Côté, René – Laval, Quebec
Coulter, L. A.
Council for Canadian Unity – Montreal, Quebec
Council of Christian Reformed Churches in Canada –
 Burlington, Ontario
Council for Exceptional Children, Quebec Chapter No. 475
 – Quebec, Quebec
Council of India Societies of Edmonton – Edmonton, Alberta
Council of Muslim Communities of Canada – Ottawa, Ontario
Council of National Ethnocultural Organizations of Canada –
 Toronto, Ontario
Council of the Quatsino Band – Quatsino Subdivision No. 18
 – British Columbia
Council of Quebec Minorities – Montreal, Quebec
Council of the Skookumchuck Band – Mission,
 British Columbia
Council for Yukon Indians – Whitehorse, Yukon
Cousins, Fred T. – Calgary, Alberta
Coutts, Thelma – Powassan, Ontario
Covey, W. – Chilliwack, British Columbia
Cowichan Band Council – Duncan, British Columbia
Coxan, Laura – Milverton, Ontario
Crawford-Craft, Hazel – Toronto, Ontario
Creed, George E. – Stoney Creek, Ontario
Creighton, Mary Martha – Tantallon, Nova Scotia
Crow, Stanley – Don Mills, Ontario
Crowe, Dolores – Saskatoon, Saskatchewan
Curran, Thomas H. – Halifax, Nova Scotia
Currie, D. V. – Edmonton, Alberta
Currier, N. – Nanaimo, British Columbia
Czechoslovak Ethnic Community – Edmonton, Alberta

D
Daigle, Kathleen B. – Whitby, Ontario
Daigle, Yvon – Sherbrooke, Quebec

Dalcourt, Madeleine – Fenwick, Ontario
Danskin, Ruby – Burnaby, British Columbia
Darrach, Ian G. – Halifax, Nova Scotia
Davis, Jack – Victoria, British Columbia
Dawe, Douglas – Ottawa, Ontario
Dawe, H. W. – Ottawa, Ontario
Day, Jean – Sarnia, Ontario
Dean, Lewis – Halifax, Nova Scotia
Degoey, Josephine – Leamington, Ontario
Dekler, David – Ottawa, Ontario
Dejesus, John M. – North Vancouver, British Columbia
de Lasala, Jennifer – Ottawa, Ontario
de Net, Va – Delhi
Denominational Education Committee of Newfoundland –
    St. John's, Newfoundland
den Ouden, Marco – Coquitlam, British Columbia
Diebe, W. – Heffley Creek, British Columbia
Dignity Canada Dignité – Winnipeg, Manitoba
Dignity Edmonton Dignité – Edmonton, Alberta
Dignity Ottawa Dignité – Ottawa, Ontario
Dinnide, Howard – Weston, Ontario
Dinniwell, Donna – London, Ontario
Dion, Léon – Quebec, Quebec
Dionne, Albert – Ste-Foy, Quebec
Dionne, François – Cap-Rouge, Quebec
Direction jeunesse – Ottawa, Ontario
Divertissements Emprise Inc. – Montreal, Quebec
Doherty, M.M. – Penetanguishene, Ontario
Doig River Band Fort St. John & Prince George District –
    Doig River Reserve, British Columbia
The Dominion of Canada English Speaking Association –
    Dorchester, New Brunswick
Dominion of Canada Party – Calgary, Alberta
Donald, G. Cameron – Edmonton, Alberta
Doswell, James W. – Oshawa, Ontario
Doull, J. A. – Halifax, Nova Scotia
Dove, Elizabeth – Kingston, Ontario
Drewer, J. – Edmonton, Alberta
Driedger, Elmer A. – Ottawa, Ontario
Duda, Michael – Halifax, Nova Scotia
Duffy, Rena – Willowdale, Ontario
Duguid, Alan T. – Calgary, Alberta
Dumontet, Elizabeth – Saskatoon, Saskatchewan
Dunbarton-Fairport United Church – Pickering, Ontario
Duncan, MacDonald W. – London, Ontario
Dunne, Patrick B. – St. John's, Newfoundland
Duriez, Donald G. – Whitehorse, Yukon
Dyck, John E. – Halifax, Nova Scotia

E
Eastman Wynne – Waterloo, Ontario
Eayrs, Jonathan – Halifax, Nova Scotia

Edmonds, Hilda L. – Edmonton, Alberta

Edwards, David R. – Consort, Alberta

Egerton Baptist Church – London Ontario

Église La Mission Chrétienne Évangélique – Sainte-Julie-de-Verchères, Quebec

Eley, L. S. – Regina, Saskatchewan

Ellis, G. L. T. – Stevensville, Ontario

Ellis, John – Hamilton, Ontario

Emberley, Kenneth – Winnipeg, Manitoba

Emergency Committee for the Defence of Religious Rights – Guelph, Ontario

Empire Loyalists Association (Governor Simcoe Branch) – Toronto, Ontario

Employers' Council of British Columbia – Vancouver, British Columbia

Employers' Council of Quebec – Montreal, Quebec

The Engineering Institute of Canada and its Constituent Societies – Montreal, Quebec

English, F. W. – Trail, British Columbia

Enright, E. Marie – Saskatoon, Saskatchewan

Ermacora, Marco – Montreal, Quebec

Esmonde-White, Robin – Charlottetown, Prince Edward Island

Etienne, Cindy – Cache Creek, British Columbia

Etienne, Gerald – Cache Creek, British Columbia

Euverman, Anne – Salmon Arm, British Columbia

Evans, Bernard – Yarker, Ontario

Evans, Helga – Coquitlam, British Columbia

Evans, Lucylle E. – Vancouver, British Columbia

Evans, W. D. – Calgary, Alberta

"L'Express de la Constitution" – Ottawa, Ontario

F

Falconer, H. M. – Toronto, Ontario

Falconer, Janet – Chase, British Columbia

The Family Life Bureau – St. John's, Newfoundland

The Fane of the Psilocybe Mushroom – Victoria, British Columbia

Farrell, James H. – Toronto, Ontario

Faucher, Jean-Charles – Outremont, Quebec

Fearn, Gordon, F. N. – Edmonton, Alberta

Federated Anti-Poverty Group of B. C. – Abbotsford, British Columbia

Federated Women's Institutes of Canada – Ottawa, Ontario

La Fédération des Associations de Parents et d'Instituteurs de Langue Française d'Ontario – Ottawa, Ontario

La Fédération des Femmes Canadiennes-Françaises – Oshawa, Ontario

La Fédération des Francophones Hors Québec – Ottawa, Ontario

Federation of Canadian Municipalities – Ottawa, Ontario

Federation of Catholic Parent-Teacher Associations of
Ontario – Ottawa, Ontario
The Federation of Chinese Canadian Professionals
(Ontario) – Toronto, Ontario
Federation of Independent Schools in Canada – Vancouver,
British Columbia
Federation of Saskatchewan Indians – Prince Albert,
Saskatchewan
Felhaleer, Carl (Mrs.) – Leamington, Ontario
Felsen, Marjorie – Victoria, British Columbia
Ferguson, Hugh J. – Chesley, Ontario
Fernandes, B. L. – Scarborough, Ontario
Ferrazzi, Giuseppe – Cambridge, Ontario
Fields, Harvey J. (Rabbi) – Toronto, Ontario
Filips, J. E. – Vancouver, British Columbia
Filliter, David F. – St-John, New Brunswick
Finlayson, R. – Scarborough, Ontario
Finnish-Canadian Cultural Federation – Toronto, Ontario
Fish, J. R. – Calgary, Alberta
Fisher, Gabriella Du Vernet – Toronto, Ontario
Fitzmaurice, Peter J. – Bracebridge, Ontario
Fleming, M. L. – Midnapau, Alberta
Flis, Jesse P. – Ottawa, Ontario
Ford, Austin H. – Calgary, Alberta
Ford, Barbara A. – Calgary, Alberta
Ford, Dorothy – Brooks, Alberta
Forest, Georges – Saint-Boniface, Manitoba
Forsey, Eugene A. – Ottawa, Ontario
Forsyth, Margaret – Wolfville, Nova Scotia
Fortier, Jacques – Ste-Foy, Quebec
Fowler, Wendy P. – Oakville, Ontario
Fox, Jean G. – Calgary, Alberta
Fraser, Carol M. – Calgary, Alberta
Fraser, John A. (Hon.) – Ottawa, Ontario
Fraser Lake Band – Fort Fraser, British Columbia
Fraser, Lewis Mr. & Mrs. – Mississauga, Ontario
Fraser, Neil A. – Sydenham, Ontario
Freedom of Choice Movement – Montreal, Quebec
Freedom of Choice Party – Montreal, Quebec
Freeman, R. F. – Ottawa, Ontario
French Association of Ontario School Boards – Ottawa,
Ontario
Frey, John – Edmonton, Alberta
Frieser, Ann – Steinbach, Manitoba
Fulcher, James S. – Ottawa, Ontario
Furlong, T. E. – St. John's, Newfoundland

G

Gaasenbeck, Karen B. – London, Ontario
Gambit Games – Chatham, Ontario
Garahan, Jim & Kathie – New Liskeard, Ontario
Gardner, J. Y. – Peackland, British Columbia

Garland, J. M. Boyd – Regina, Saskatchewan
Garrison, Philip – Montreal, Quebec
Gaspire, Cyril & Marina – St. Thomas, Ontario
Gay Fathers of Toronto – Toronto, Ontario
Gentry, Peter – Petawawa, Ontario
Geraets, Théodore F. – Ottawa, Ontario
The German Canadian Club of Red Deer – Red Deer, Alberta
German-Canadian Committee on the Constitution – Ottawa,
    Ontario
Gibson, Alan J. – Calgary, Alberta
Gibson, Everett – Powassan, Ontario
Gibson, Gertrude – Powassan, Ontario
Gierutto, Helena – Toronto, Ontario
Gilbert, Marc – Montreal, Quebec
Gillate, Sidney F. – Penticton, British Columbia
Gilley, Donald R. – Calgary, Alberta
Gitanmaax Band Council – Hazelton, British Columbia
Gitksan-Carrier Tribal Council – Hazelton, British Columbia
Glass, J. G. – Calgary, Alberta
Goddard, Ruth – Cambridge, Ontario
Goddard, Teresa – Cambridge, Ontario
Godwin, G. – Calgary, Alberta
Good, I. – Cambridge, Ontario
Gordon, Bill – Calgary, Alberta
Gordon, Frances – Calgary, Alberta
Gorman, Ruth – Calgary, Alberta
Gorman, Ruth (Dr.) – Calgary, Alberta
Goulden, L. N. – Edmonton, Alberta
Gouvernement du Québec Constitution Express No. 2,
    No. 3 – Quebec, Quebec
Government of Alberta – Edmonton, Alberta
Government of British Columbia – Victoria, British Columbia
Government of New Brunswick – Fredericton, New Brunswick
Government of Manitoba – Winnipeg, Manitoba
Government of the Northwest Territories – Yellowknife,
    Northwest Territories
Government of Nova Scotia – Halifax, Nova Scotia
Government of Prince Edward Island – Charlottetown,
    Prince Edward Island
Government of Saskatchewan – Regina, Saskatchewan
Government of Yukon – Whitehorse, Yukon
Gralnoski, Joseph A. – Powassan, Ontario
Grand Council Treaty No. 3 – Kenora, Ontario
Grand Council Treaty No. 9 – Timmins, Ontario
Grand Orange Lodge of Canada – Fredericton,
    New Brunswick
Grant, Hugh – Toronto, Ontario
Graves, Joseph – Hamilton, Ontario
Grayson, Thomas B. – Scarborough, Ontario
Green, Sidney – Winnipeg, Manitoba
Greene, Ian – Parson, British Columbia
Greenfield, Robert S. – Metcalfe, Ontario

Greenwood, F. Murray – Vancouver, British Columbia
Griffiths, Ruth – Prince Albert, Saskatchewan
Grolle, E. Hendrik – Regina, Saskatchewan
Group for Survival – Saskatoon, Saskatchewan
Grygier, Tadeusz – Ottawa, Ontario
Guttne, Nancy – Calgary, Alberta

H

Haddock, Yoland – Fernie, British Columbia
Hagwilget Band Council – New Hazelton, British Columbia
Hall, Fred – Longbow Lake Post Office, Ontario
Hall, Terry – Ottawa, Ontario
Hamilton, Ernest – Forthill, Ontario
Hamilton, Elinor – Forthill, Ontario
Hamilton, Gordon – Kelowna, British Columbia
Hamilton, W. D. – Fredericton, New Brunswick
Hammond, Jessie L. – West Vancouver, British Columbia
Hann, Ray – Winnipeg, Manitoba
Hansen, Albert – Wasaga Beach, Ontario
Hanson, Brian – Calgary, Alberta
Harder, Agatha – Ottawa, Ontario
Harder, Cornelius – Ottawa, Ontario
Hardy, Helen – Toronto, Ontario
Harris, William – London, Ontario
Hart, S. W. D. – Picton, Ontario
Hart, W. J. – Willowdale, Ontario
Harvie, André – Calgary, Alberta
Hatfield, H. R. – Penticton, British Columbia
Hauck, Margaret – Kitchener, Ontario
Hawkesworth, Bob – Calgary, Alberta
Haworth, D. – Aurora, Ontario
Hay, Joan A. – Port Alberni, British Columbia
Hay, W. – Winnipeg, Manitoba
Hayward, R. B. – Halifax, Nova Scotia
Heeney, Dennis H. – Brandon, Manitoba
Henderson, Anna – Toronto, Ontario
Henderson, Luci – Duntroon, Ontario
Hennessy, Peter H. – Elginburg, Ontario
Henry, Penny – Vedder Crossing, British Columbia
Herring, Joyce – Calgary, Alberta
Higgins, Catherine L. – Islington, Ontario
Higgins, Catherine M. – Islington, Ontario
Higgins, Jerome – Islington, Ontario
Higgins, John A. – Islington, Ontario
Higgins, John P. – Islington, Ontario
Higgins, Mary Jane – Islington, Ontario
Hill, James Thomas – Sudbury, Ontario
Hillyer, Fred – Cardston, Alberta
Hind, M. – Calgary, Alberta
Hind, Peter – Calgary, Alberta
Hodgins, Barbara L. – Calgary, Alberta
Hodgson, W. George – Lindsay, Ontario

Hogan, William (Mrs.) – Powassan, Ontario
Hogg, Peter W. – Downsview, Ontario
Hogg, R. – Kelowna, British Columbia
Hollinger, Benjamin – Pembroke, Ontario
Holmes, Mildred V. – Sutton West, Ontario
Holy, Mary – Pickering, Ontario
Hooten, J. A. – Calgary, Alberta
Hooten, Maureen – Calgary, Alberta
Hooten, N. R. – Calgary, Alberta
Horton, Harry – Windsor, Ontario
Hough, Barbara J. – Halifax, Nova Scotia
Houle, Patricia – Sarnia, Ontario
Howard, Susan A. – Sarnia, Ontario
Howard, T. P. – Calgary, Alberta
Howden, Peter H. – Barrie, Ontario
Howe, Glen – Toronto, Ontario
Hubka, Brian F. – Coleman, Alberta
Hubscher, Frank Fred – Toronto, Ontario
Hughes, Ken – Edmonton, Alberta
Human Action to Limit Taxes (HALT) – Vancouver, British
  Columbia
Human Rights Institute of Canada – Ottawa, Ontario
Hummel, Dorothy – Powassan, Ontario
Hummel, Joe – Powassan, Ontario
Humphries, A. J. – Vancouver, British Columbia
Hunt, Glenda – Red Deer, Alberta
Hunt, G. Patrick – Mount Uniacke, Nova Scotia
Hunter, Allan D. – Calgary, Alberta
Husby, Philip J. – Winnipeg, Manitoba
Hutchings, Gertrude – High River, Alberta
Hypher, R. P. – Carrying Place, Ontario

I

Ibbitson, Clayton – Powassan, Ontario
Ibbitson, Jean – Powassan, Ontario
Iervella, Silvana – Calgary, Alberta
Ifejika, Samuel U. – Toronto, Ontario
Indian Association of Alberta – Edmonton, Alberta
Indian Constitution Express – Ottawa, Ontario
Indian Rights for Indian Women – Edmonton, Alberta
Indo-Canadian Society of Alberta – Edmonton, Alberta
Info Pop – Montreal, Quebec
Innes, Eugene W. – Regina, Saskatchewan
International Council of Sikhs – Toronto, Ontario
The International Ombudsman Institute – Edmonton, Alberta
Inuit Committee on National Issues – Ottawa, Ontario
Ireland, V. – Toronto, Ontario
Irvin, George – Dorchester, Ontario
Ivanochko, Bob – Regina, Saskatchewan
Iwanus, Jaroslaw (Jerry) – Edmonton, Alberta

J

Jackson, Arthur S. – Ottawa, Ontario
Jackson, F. L. – St. John's, Newfoundland
Jacob, O. – Oshawa, Ontario
Jaeger, Martin – Toronto, Ontario
James, Norman G. – Burlington, Ontario
Janda, Richard A. – Toronto, Ontario
Jansen, Russell – Kelowna, British Columbia
Jarionsynski, Witold – Warszawa, Poland
Jewitt, Brian – Ottawa, Ontario
Jimmie, Sam – Sardis, British Columbia
Johnson, Calven – Estevan, Saskatchewan
Johnson, Chris – St. John, New Brunswick
Johnson, H. S. – Oakville, Ontario
Johnston, Terry L. – Edmonton, Alberta
Johnston, William C. – Burlington, Ontario
Johnstone, D. G. – Hamilton, Ontario
Jones, David G. – Fort McMurray, Alberta
Jones, T. P. – Ottawa, Ontario
Jorlin, Don – Calgary, Alberta
Joynt, C. S. – Calgary, Alberta
Judd, Anne – Port Elgin, Ontario
Julia, Sister M. – London, Ontario
Julian, Glenn E. – Kitchener, Ontario

K

Kabut, Ursula – Brooks, Alberta
Kaiser, K. – Edmonton, Alberta
Kallion, R. – Thunder Bay, Ontario
Kane, Cecce – Salmon Arm, British Columbia
Kane, Sally – Salmon Arm, British Columbia
Kay, Roy – New Westminster, British Columbia
Kear, A. R. – Winnipeg, Manitoba
Keevil, Scott – Oakville, Ontario
Kelly, Allan A. – Thunder Bay, Ontario
Kelly, Margaret – Trout Creek, Ontario
Kelly, Mary – Powassan, Ontario
Kelly, Maureen – London, Ontario
Kemp, Fred D. V. – Calgary, Alberta
Kennedy, Michael P. J. – Saskatoon, Saskatchewan
Kennedy, Sean M. – Montreal, Quebec
Kennedy, Jackson, Irlma – Hamilton, Ontario
Kent, Alan – Toronto, Ontario
Kerigan, A. T. – Hamilton, Ontario
Kerr, A. C. (Mr. & Mrs.) – Burnaby, British Columbia
Kerr, Peter – Victoria, British Columbia
Kerr, Robert W. – Windsor, Ontario
Kieffer, Virginia – Teeswater, Ontario
Kiesman, Clarence – Moosehorn, Manitoba
Killoran, M. Maureen – Hamilton, Ontario
Kim, Mary-Ann – Nepean, Ontario
King, Vivian – Montreal, Quebec

Kirton, N. G. – Calgary, Alberta
Kitchen, Kathryn A. – Cambridge, Ontario
Klarer, Allen – Oakville, Ontario
Klein, Ralph – Calgary, Alberta
Klenman, Norman – Vancouver, British Columbia
Knapp, Bruce H. – Peterborough, Ontario
Knelman, F. H. – Montreal, Quebec
Knights of Columbus (Council 1007) – North Bay, Ontario
Knights of Columbus (Council 1916) – Renfrew, Ontario
Knights of Columbus (Council 2082) – Arnprior, Ontario
Knights of Columbus (Father Doyle Council No. 6745)
    – Mount Forest, Ontario
Knights of Columbus (Francis Lemieux Council No. 6388)
    – Longlac, Ontario
Knights of Columbus (Marian Council No. 3881) – Oakville,
    Ontario
Knights of Columbus (Sacred Heart Council 4120) –
    Tottenham, Ontario
Kocsis, William – Port Stanley, Ontario
Koning, Jean (Mrs.) – Oldcastle, Ontario
Kootenay Indian Area Council – Cranbrook, British Columbia
Korey, George – Toronto, Ontario
Kostuchuk, J. A. – Dauphin, Manitoba
Kowal, Donald – Kingston, Ontario
Kraemer, Anne – Walkerton, Ontario
Kraemer, J. Edward – Walkerton, Ontario
Krenz, Cecil – Saskatoon, Saskatchewan
Kuhn, Bernie – St. Thomas, Ontario
Kulmar, E. – Weston, Ontario
Kumar, Prem – Edmonton, Alberta

L
LaBerge, Dan – Newcastle, New Brunswick
La Branche, Richard – Montreal, Quebec
Lac La Biche Chamber of Commerce – Lac La Biche, Alberta
Ladouceur, Yvonne – Montreal, Quebec
Lafleur, François – Ste-Foy, Quebec
LaForest, Gérard G. V. – Ottawa, Ontario
Laichkwitach State Tribes – Campbell River, British
    Columbia
Langevin, Celia – Niagara Falls, Ontario
Lapierre, Laurette – Boucherville, Quebec
Lapierre, Yvette – Boucherville, Quebec
Lapp, M. A. – Calgary, Alberta
La Prairie, Vicki – Aylmer Lucerne, Quebec
Larisey, Don – Carleton Place, Ontario
Lauriault, Gary Anthony – Orléans, Ontario
Lavoie, Marie E. – Calgary, Alberta
Laurence, Marilyn L. – Toronto, Ontario
Lawrence, Ross D. – Willowdale, Ontario
Lawson, A. (Mrs.) – Duchess, Alberta
Lawson, Ina – Thunder Bay, Ontario

The Law Union of British Columbia – Vancouver,
  British Columbia
Laxdal, Walter V. G. – Saskatoon, Saskatchewan
Layman, Pauline – Victoria, British Columbia
Leahy, J. H. – Powassan, Ontario
Leblanc, Sylvio – Cornwall, Ontario
LeBreton, Emilien – Lower Neguac, New Brunswick
Lécuyer, André – Don Mills, Ontario
Lederman, W. R. – Kingston, Ontario
Lee, John C. – St. Catharines, Ontario
Lee-Paget, D. J. – Winnipeg, Manitoba
Leeder, C. E. – Grimsby, Ontario
Leier, Dale Philip – Lethbridge, Alberta
Leighton, Lynn – Markham, Ontario
Leitch, Pauline D. – Thornhill, Ontario
Lemieux, Joseph-Paul-Émile – Mont-Louis, Comté Gaspé,
  Quebec
Lemire, Sister Mary Carol – Willowdale, Ontario
Lentsch, John J. – Delta, British Columbia
Leon, Robert – Toronto, Ontario
Leuheoct, Biel – Okotoks, Alberta
Levert, J. Raymond – Mississauga, Ontario
Levi, John – Pakenham, Ontario
Leymen, Ken – Vancouver, British Columbia
Lieb, Randy – Swift Current, Saskatchewan
Lippect, Frank – Chepston, Ontario
Lipsett, Edwart H. – Winnipeg, Manitoba
Little, Nina – Vancouver, British Columbia
Lockhart, Andy – Calgary, Alberta
Lockwood, Bette – Calgary, Alberta
Logan, Brian James – Edmonton, Alberta
Logan, Lola – Edmonton, Alberta
London & Middlesex County Roman Catholic Separate
  School Board – London, Ontario
Long, E. P. M. – Sidney, British Columbia
Longmore, Elizabeth – Calgary, Alberta
Looyen, C. D. – Surrey, British Columbia
Looyen, Claire – Surrey, British Columbia
Lopez, Alicia – St. Thomas, Ontario
Loring, Marian O. – Tangent, Alberta
Lott, David – Ganges, British Columbia
Loughran, Hugh – Mississauga, Ontario
Loughran, Patricia – Mississauga, Ontario
Love, D. V. – Toronto, Ontario
Lovett, Frank J. (Mr. & Mrs.) – Willowdale, Ontario
Lowen, Amy E. – Maple Ridge, British Columbia
Lower Nicola Band – Merritt, British Columbia
Lozanski, Walter R. – Calgary, Alberta
Ludlow, Dennis W. – Don Mills, Ontario
Lussier, Michel – Montreal, Quebec
Lynch, Mike – St. Thomas, Ontario

Lyon, Noel – Kingston, Ontario
Lyons, Robert – Toronto, Ontario
Lysyk, Kenneth M. – Vancouver, British Columbia

M

MacKay, A. Wayne – Halifax, Nova Scotia
MacKenzie, Norma S. – Downsview, Ontario
MacKinnon, J. C. – Saskatoon, Saskatchewan
MacLean, John B. – Kingston, Ontario
MacNeil, Malcolm H. – Fredericton, New Brunswick
MacNeill, Dorothy – Port Hawkesbury, Nova Scotia
Macpherson, Jean (Mrs.) – Toronto, Ontario
Madden, Wayne D. – Fort McMurray, Alberta
Magee, D. E. – Barrie, Ontario
Mahaffy, Earle F. – Calgary, Alberta
Mahoney, A. P. (Rev.) – London, Ontario
Malloway, Kathy – Sardis, British Columbia
Malloway, Tony – Sardis, British Columbia
Maloney, Beverley – Marmora, Ontario
Manis, Vincent – Vancouver, British Columbia
Manitoba Association for Rights and Liberties – Winnipeg,
    Manitoba
Manitoba Association of Friendship Centres Inc. – Winnipeg,
    Manitoba
Manitoba Association of Women and the Law – Winnipeg,
    Manitoba
Manitoba Law Union – Winnipeg, Manitoba
Manitoba Office of the Ombudsman – Winnipeg, Manitoba
Manitoba Parents for Ukrainian Education Inc. – Winnipeg,
    Manitoba
Mannan, A. – Winnipeg, Manitoba
Mannock, David – Vancouver, British Columbia
Manor, Robert – Vancouver, British Columbia
Manson, Mr. & Mrs. – Calgary, Alberta
Maoney, Monica – Saint John, New Brunswick
Marshall, Hilda A. J. – Victoria, British Columbia
Martin, L. J. – Calgary, Alberta
Martin, Paul – St. Jacobs, Ontario
Martin, Sandra – Toronto, Ontario
The Marxist-Leninist Organization of Canada
Mascotto, Adrien William – Geraldton, Ontario
Maskell, Fred G. B. – Ottawa, Ontario
Maskell, Monica, M. F. – Ottawa, Ontario
Mason, Clyde D. – Halifax, Nova Scotia
Mason, Kenneth H. – Dutton, Ontario
Masschaele, James – London, Ontario
Masterson, Brennan F. – Scarborough, Ontario
Maten, Steve – St. Bruno, Quebec
Matheson, Douglas R. – Edmonton, Alberta
Mathewson, Donald H. – Calgary, Alberta
Matsubara, Mark M. – Ottawa, Ontario
Matte, Louis J. – Prince George, British Columbia

Matthews, Norman H. – Maple, Ontario
McAllister, Irene L. – Vancouver, British Columbia
McArthur, D. A. – Guelph, Ontario
McAuley, Daniel L. – Toronto, Ontario
McCaldon, R. J. – Kingston, Ontario
McCall, Gil – Quesnel, British Columbia
McCamis, J. G. – Calgary, Alberta
McCarthy, Farrell – Newcastle, New Brunswick
McCatty, S. A. – Nepean, Ontario
McComb, Albert – Toronto, Ontario
McCormack, Susan – Vancouver, British Columbia
McCraw, Claire – St. Thomas, Ontario
McCreery, K. J. – Milton, Ontario
McDonald, Robert – Montreal, Quebec
McDonald, Virginia – Downsview, Ontario
McDonell, John – Kirkland Lake, Ontario
McDougall, Hugh – Weston, Ontario
McDougall, Gloria – Weston, Ontario
McFadyen, Kevin – Edmonton, Alberta
McFee, Harry F. – Winnipeg, Manitoba
McGillivray, A. B. – Calgary, Alberta
McGirr, James – Brampton, Ontario
McIntosh, Trudy – Sarnia, Ontario
McIntyre, E. – Windsor, Ontario
McIsaac, H. (Mr. & Mrs.) – Sudbury, Ontario
McKenzie, Gerald F. – Ajax, Ontario
McKeon, Charles F. – Toronto, Ontario
McKinney, Norman – Toronto, Ontario
McLaughlin, Robert N. – Toronto, Ontario
McLellan, Brian James – Sarnia, Ontario
McLeod, Leona, A. – Victoria, British Columbia
McLeod, R. A. – Victoria, British Columbia
McMullen, Norman – Willowdale, Ontario
McNally, Harold – Willowdale, Ontario
McNally, Margaret – Willowdale, Ontario
McNamee, J. J. – New Liskeard, Ontario
McNee, James D. – Brandon, Manitoba
McNulty, Yolande – Oshawa, Ontario
McPhedran, A. – Calgary, Alberta
McRuer, J. C. – Toronto, Ontario
McWhinney, Edward – Vancouver, British Columbia
Media Club of Canada – Saint John, New Brunswick
Mennonite Central Committee (Canada) – Ottawa, Ontario
Mercer, John S. – Toronto, Ontario
Mérey, Pamela – Toronto, Ontario
Mérey, Peter – Toronto, Ontario
Metis Association of Alberta – Edmonton, Alberta
Metropolitan Separate School Board – Toronto, Ontario
Mewett, Alan W. – Toronto, Ontario
Michalski, C. – Camden East, Ontario
Michalski, W. – Camden East, Ontario
Michaud, Victoria – Powassan, Ontario

Michefske, Martha – Powassan, Ontario
Miles, Robert – Kelowna, British Columbia
Millar, R. C. – Otterburn Park, Quebec
Millen, William – Teeswater, Ontario
Miller, Mary Jane – St. Catharines, Ontario
Miller, Norman W. – Calgary, Alberta
Miller, Wes – Burlington, Ontario
Milner, Betty – Calgary, Alberta
The Mining Association of Canada – Ottawa, Ontario
The Minority Rights Group – Oakville, Ontario
Miskokoman, Roberta – Muncey, Ontario
Mitchell, Andrew S. – Sidney, British Columbia
Mitchell, Doris I. – Sault Ste. Marie, Ontario
Mitchell, Marcelle – Ottawa, Ontario
Mitchell, Osborne – Victoria, British Columbia
Miyata, T. – Atikokan, Ontario
Mohawk Council of Kahnawake – Kahnawake, Quebec
Molfora, Giovanni (and Group) – Montreal, Quebec
Moore, J. Sherrold – Calgary, Alberta
Moore, John L. – Vancouver, British Columbia
Morel, François – Ste-Foy, Quebec
Morgan, David – Halifax, Nova Scotia
Morgan, W. O. – Vancouver, British Columbia
Moriarity, Linda – Calgary, Alberta
Morrow, W. R. – Calgary, Alberta
Morton, Ralph – Cowichan Bay, British Columbia
Mountain, Elizabeth (Beth) – Willowdale, Ontario
Mountain, Howard R. J. – Willowdale, Ontario
Mowers, Cleo W. – Lethbridge, Alberta
Muckle, Marjorie E. – Mississauga, Ontario
Muise, Leonard – Stephenville, Newfoundland
Multicultural Association of Fredericton Inc. – Fredericton,
    New Brunswick
Multilingual Association of Regina Inc. – Regina,
    Saskatchewan
Munroe, Isabel A. – Edmonton, Alberta
Murduff, C. (Mrs.) – Peterborough, Ontario
Murphy, D. P. – Agincourt, Ontario
Murphy, Rhoda – Calgary, Alberta
Murphy, Sandra – St. Thomas, Ontario
Murray, David C. – Guelph, Ontario
Murray, Jim – North Vancouver, British Columbia
Musial, Frederich A. – Atlin, British Columbia
Muttart, Margaret W. – Summerside, Prince Edward Island

N
NACHES Montreal's Gay Jewish Group – Montreal, Quebec
Nadeau, Sauveur – Oshawa, Ontario
Nagel, Rudy – Toronto, Ontario
Nalli, Mary – Mississauga, Ontario
Naphin, Robert L. – Saskatoon, Saskatchewan
Nash, David (Mr. & Mrs.) – Fort Erie, Ontario

Nassivera, T. (Ms) – Toronto, Ontario

National Action Committee on the Status of Women –
Toronto, Ontario

National Anti-Poverty Organization N.A.P.O. – Ottawa,
Ontario

National Association of Canadians of Origins in India,
(NACOI) – Ottawa, Ontario

National Association of Japanese Canadians – Vancouver,
British Columbia

The National Association of Women and the Law
(N.A.W.L.) – Ottawa, Ontario

The National Black Coalition of Canada – Willowdale,
Ontario

National Chapter of Canada IODE (Provincial Chapter of
New Brunswick IODE) – Toronto, Ontario

National Citizens' Coalition – Toronto, Ontario

National Committee for Language Equality (NCLE) –
Montreal, Quebec

National Italian-Canadian Congress, Quebec Region –
Montreal, Quebec

National Council of Jewish Women of Canada – Downsview,
Ontario

The National Council of Women of Canada – Ottawa,
Ontario

National Farmers Union – Saskatoon, Saskatchewan

National Firearms Association, New Brunswick Branch –
Woodstock, New Brunswick

National Indian Brotherhood – Ottawa, Ontario

National Indian Brotherhood, Chiefs of Treaty No. 7, Tribes
of Alberta – Ottawa, Ontario

The National Pensioners and Senior Citizens Federation –
Toronto, Ontario

Native Brotherhood of British Columbia – Vancouver,
British Columbia

Native Council of Canada (Métis and Non-Status Indians) –
Ottawa, Ontario

Native Peoples Resource Centre – London, Ontario

The Native Rights Coalition – Regina, Saskatchewan

Native Women's Association of Canada – Ottawa, Ontario

Nattrass, Eileen – Victoria, British Columbia

Nederend, Joanne – Breslau, Ontario

Nelson, N. V. – Prince George, British Columbia

Nelson, Ruben F. W. – Ottawa, Ontario

Nemiah Valley Band – Nemiah Valley, British Columbia

New Brunswick Association for the Advancement of Coloured
People – Saint John, New Brunswick

The New Brunswick Development Institute – Fredericton,
New Brunswick

The New Brunswick Human Rights Commission –
Fredericton, New Brunswick

New Brunswick Right to Life Association – Moncton, New
Brunswick

Newby, Hester – Niagara Falls, Ontario
New Democratic Party of Newfoundland & Labrador –
	Corner Brook, Newfoundland
Nichol, Margaret J. – Markham, Ontario
Nicholas, Peter – Trenton, Ontario
Nicholas, S. M. – Calgary, Alberta
Nicholls, Peter – St. Catharines, Ontario
Nicholson, Arthur Gwyn – Orleans, Ontario
Nishga Tribal Council – New Aiyansh, British Columbia
Noble, K. W. – Ottawa, Ontario
Nolet, Richard – Sault Ste-Marie, Ontario
Nooaitch Indian Reserve – Merritt, British Columbia
North Shore Liberal Women – West Vancouver,
	British Columbia
North Shore Women's Centre – North Vancouver,
	British Columbia
The Nova Scotia Network of CCLOW – Dartmouth,
	Nova Scotia
Nova Scotia Real Estate Association – Halifax, Nova Scotia
Nowlan, Michel – Ville d'Anjou, Quebec
Nuu-Chah-Nulth Tribal Council – Vancouver Island,
	British Columbia

O

Oakley, Elsie – Thamesford, Ontario
O'Brien, Edward – Toronto, Ontario
O'Brien, Margaret – Scarborough, Ontario
O'Connell, William J. – Don Mills, Ontario
O'Connor, Liz – St. Thomas, Ontario
O'Connor, T. Peter – Calgary, Alberta
O'Farrell – Ste-Foy, Quebec
O'Hearn, P. J. T. – Halifax, Nova Scotia
Ohlheiser, Sandra – Champion, Alberta
Olenick, Roberta – Vancouver, British Columbia
O'Neill, Mary – Islington, Ontario
The Ontario Committee on the Status of Women – Toronto,
	Ontario
The Ontario Conference of Catholic Bishops – Toronto,
	Ontario
Ontario English Catholic Teachers' Association – Toronto,
	Ontario
The Ontario Federation of Anglers & Hunters –
	Peterborough, Ontario
Ontario Human Rights Commission – Toronto, Ontario
Ontario Progressive Conservative Association of Women –
	Cornwall, Ontario
Ontario Separate School Trustees' Association – Willowdale,
	Ontario
Ontario Welfare Council – Toronto, Ontario
Operation Dismantle – Ottawa, Ontario
Organization for Caribbean Canadian Initiatives –
	Willowdale, Ontario

Oromocto, Town of – Oromocto, New Brunswick
Orr, A. W. – Calgary, Alberta
O'Shaughnessy, John – Powassan, Ontario
O'Shea, Patrick (Mr. & Mrs.) – Rexdale, Ontario
The Ottawa Board of Education – Ottawa, Ontario
Ottenbrite, K. – Bramalea, Ontario
Our Lady of the Airways – Mississauga, Ontario
Owens, Susan – Powassan, Ontario

P
Pacific Vocational Institute – Burnaby, British Columbia
Palmer, John R. N. – Orillia, Ontario
Parent Finders Incorporated – Willowdale, Ontario
Park, Marvin – Canfield, Ontario
Parkman, Cathy – Charlottetown, Prince Edward Island
The Pas Indian Band – The Pas, Manitoba
Paterson, M. – Calgary, Alberta
Paterson, W. – Calgary, Alberta
Patterson, A. M. – Calgary, Alberta
Patterson, Kathleen A. – West Vancouver, British Columbia
Pavilion Indian Band – Cache Creek, British Columbia
Pawih, Jack – Cartwright, Manitoba
Payne, Dexter, K. – Kentville, Nova Scotia
Pearson, George – Lindsay, Ontario
Peel Sharpshooters – Brampton, Ontario
Peet, F. G. – Brentwood Bay, British Columbia
Pelech, William – Sherwood Park, Alberta
Pelerine, Carolyn – New Glasgow, Nova Scotia
Penna, Dan E. – Saskatoon, Saskatchewan
Penner, Norman – Toronto, Ontario
Penticton Indian Band – Penticton, British Columbia
The Peoples Law School Society – Vancouver, British
  Columbia
Pépin, Lorraine – Powassan, Ontario
Perras, P. William jr. – Oakville, Ontario
Perry, Dennis W. – Chester, Nova Scotia
Perry, Thomas L. jr. – Houston, British Columbia
Peterborough Libertarian Association – Peterborough, Ontario
Peters, Glendon Trevor – Saint John, New Brunswick
Petrovici, Boris – St. Catharines, Ontario
Petry, Lucien A. – Regina, Saskatchewan
Pettick, Joseph – Regina, Saskatchewan
Phillips, Wendell – Delta, British Columbia
Piekarski, Frank – Powassan, Ontario
Piekarski, Teresa – Powassan, Ontario
Piercy, Beth – London, Ontario
Pilisi, Paul – Ste-Foy, Quebec
Pinkney, R. D. – Georgetown, Ontario
Pinsonneault, Rolland – Regina, Saskatchewan
Pitre-Lefebvre, Florence – Saint Albert, Alberta
Planned Parenthood Federation of Canada – Ottawa, Ontario
Plante, Frank – Windsor, Ontario

Plumley, George – Guelph, Ontario

Podger, Robert J. – Toronto, Ontario

Poechman, Gerald P. – Walkerton, Ontario

Pollock, Nancy – Willowdale, Ontario

Poncelet, Maurice – Ottawa, Ontario

Pope, A. C. – Toronto, Ontario

The Port Coquitlam Area Women's Centre – Port Coquitlam,
   British Columbia

Porteous, James – Willowdale, Ontario

Porter, H. A. – Ottawa, Ontario

Porter, K. E. – Winnipeg, Manitoba

Port Simpson Band Council – Port Simpson, British Columbia

Positive Action Committee – Montreal, Quebec

Poulin, Gaétan – St-Agapit, Quebec

The Presbytery of Newfoundland – St. John's, Newfoundland

Prescott-Russell County Roman Catholic Separate School
   Board – L'Orignal, Ontario

Prest, Steve – Sardis, British Columbia

Pringle, W. R. – Winnipeg, Manitoba

Progressive Conservative Women's Association of North Bay –
   North Bay, Ontario

Progressive Conservative Party of Saskatchewan –
   Saskatchewan

Progressive Conservative Association of Okanagan North –
   Kelowna, British Columbia

The Protestant School Board of Greater Montreal – Montreal,
   Quebec

Provincial Association of Catholic Teachers – Montreal,
   Quebec

Provincial Progressive Conservative Association – Calgary,
   Alberta

Puddy, James & Margaret – Agincourt, Ontario

Public Interest Advocacy Centre – Ottawa, Ontario

Q

Quarry, Grace, Andrew and Robert George – Guelph, Ontario

The Quebec Committee for Language Regions – Montreal,
   Quebec

Quebec Federation of Home and School Associations –
   Montreal, Quebec

Quebecer's Labrador Association – Les Grondines, Quebec

Quesnel, Janine – Crysler, Ontario

Quigley, Robert F. – St. John's, Newfoundland

Quitner, Joe K. – Toronto, Ontario

R

Ragona, Linda – Calgary, Alberta

Rastall, Peter – Vancouver, British Columbia

Rauser, John – Mitchell, Ontario

Realty Owners of Canada – Don Mills, Ontario

Recluses Missionnaires – Montreal, Quebec

Red Pheasant Band, No. 108 – Cando, Saskatchewan

Redemptorist Fathers – Toronto, Ontario
Reed, Lorne H. – Calgary, Alberta
Regehr, Echo – Coutts, Alberta
Regehr, Jack – Coutts, Alberta
Le Regroupement pour les droits politiques du Québec
Reichert, Walter – Pilger, Saskatchewan
Reid, John S. – Cambridge, Ontario
Reinke, H. S. – Thornhill, Ontario
Religious Information Centre – Vancouver, British Columbia
The Religious Society of Friends (Quaker) – St. John's,
  Newfoundland
Rémillard, Gil – Montreal, Quebec
Renaissance Family Institute – Milton, Ontario
Renaissance International – Milton, Ontario
Renaud, J.-Claude – Gatineau, Quebec
Renault, Arlene M. – Salmon Arm, British Columbia
Richard, Ethel – Ottawa, Ontario
Rick, Alban – Powassan, Ontario
Rick, Louise – Powassan, Ontario
Right To Life – Kitchener, Ontario
Right to Life Association of Toronto and Area – Toronto,
  Ontario
Riley, K. E. – Lethbridge, Alberta
Rinck, Aksel – Weston, Ontario
Ring, Harold & Winifred – Richmond Hill, Ontario
Ringrose, E. G. – Calgary, Alberta
Ritchie, H. S. – Stratford, Ontario
Robertson, Elizabeth – Didsbury, Alberta
Robertson, H. – Stratford, Ontario
Robinson, Sharon – Edmonton, Alberta
Rodwick, Graeme – Nepean, Ontario
Rogers, Craig T. – Windsor, Ontario
Rogers, Elwyn A. – Toronto, Ontario
Rogers, Smellard, Jane Daphne – Peterborough, Ontario
Rombough, Jessie – Calgary, Alberta
Ronaghan, Allan – Winnipeg, Manitoba
Roper, Henry – Halifax, Nova Scotia
Rosenberg, Richard S. – Winnipeg, Manitoba
Ross, Romaine K. – St. Catharines, Ontario
Rossi, Carlo – Ottawa, Ontario
Rothney, Gordon – St. John College, Manitoba
Roussel, Georges – Oshawa, Ontario
Routliffe, C. D. – Mississauga, Ontario
Rowe, F. W. – Ottawa, Ontario
Roxan, Ian – Toronto, Ontario
Roy, Albert J. – Ottawa, Ontario
Roy, Gilles & Desneiges – Southampton, Ontario
The Royal Commonwealth Society – Toronto, Ontario
Rowe, Elizabeth – London, Ontario
Rudd, Theodore – Lethbridge, Alberta
Rudnyckyj, J. B. – Montreal, Quebec
Rudolph, Mildred – Lloydminster, Alberta

Ruffman, Alan – Halifax, Nova Scotia
Rundle, B. J. – Toronto, Ontario
Rurak, George – Salmon Arm, British Columbia
Russell, Hubert E. – Islington, Ontario
Russell, Peter H. – Toronto, Ontario
Rutledge, Douglas E. – Belleville, Ontario
Rutledge, Fred – Moncton, New Brunswick
Ryan, H. R. S. – Kingston, Ontario

S
St. Andrew's College in Winnipeg – Winnipeg, Manitoba
St. Boniface Catholic Women's League of Canada – Maryhill,
   Ontario
St. Clare School – Mississauga, Ontario
St. Mary's Band – Cranbrook, British Columbia
All Saints' Anglican Church – Milville, Saskatchewan
Saldov, Morris – Toronto, Ontario
Sallmen, Helen – Ottawa, Ontario
Bande Salteau No. 542 – East Moberly Lake, British
   Columbia
Sam, Mitze – Vedder Crossing, British Columbia
Sander, Joe – Saskatoon, Saskatchewan
Sander, Roy – Vauxhall, Alberta
Sanders, Douglas – Vancouver, British Columbia
Saprarolle, Gertrude – Saskatoon, Saskatchewan
Sarnia Indian Research – Sarnia, Ontario
Saskatchewan Advisory Council on the Status of Women –
   Saskatoon, Saskatchewan
Saskatchewan Human Rights Commission – Saskatoon,
   Saskatchewan
Saskatchewan Real Estate Association – Saskatoon,
   Saskatchewan
Saskatoon Catholic Schools – Saskatoon, Saskatchewan
Say, Vivian I. – Vancouver, British Columbia
Sayer, Laurie – London, Ontario
Schelvey, M. A. – London, Ontario
Schmalz, Alice – Cambridge, Ontario
School Sisters of Notre-Dame – Waterdown, Ontario
Schuetz, C. F. – Ottawa, Ontario
Schurter, Jerome – Chepstow, Ontario
Schwartz, Bryan – Ottawa, Ontario
Scott, Donald A. – Winnipeg, Manitoba
Scott, Jackie – Cupar, Saskatchewan
Scott, Len – Cupar, Saskatchewan
Scott, Stephen A. – Westmount, Quebec
Scowlitz Indian Band – Harrison Mills, British Columbia
Secor Inc. – Montreal, Quebec
Seguin-Sweeney, Denise – London, Ontario
Seidl, Peter – Vancouver, British Columbia
Senior Citizens' Central Council of Calgary – Calgary,
   Alberta
Sepass, Mona – Sardis, British Columbia

Seto, David – Chicoutimi, Quebec
Shackan Indian Band – Merritt, British Columbia
Shaw, M. A. – Calgary, Alberta
Shea, Patrick D. – Ottawa, Ontario
Shead, Bill – Selkirk, Manitoba
Shore, Martin – Victoria, British Columbia
Short, Leslie – Montreal, Quebec
Siddon, T. – Richmond, British Columbia
Silaj, Les – Elliot, British Columbia
Silver, Shoel – Toronto, Ontario
Simpson, C. H. – Kelowna, British Columbia
Simpson, W. E. – Belleville, Ontario
Sims, Anthony
Sinclair, E. Jean – Vancouver, British Columbia
Sinclair, L. R. – Vancouver, British Columbia
Sinclair, Stanley R. – Regina, Saskatchewan
Sindlinger, Tom – Edmonton, Alberta
Slattery, Brian – Saskatoon, Saskatchewan
Slovenian Canadian Association – Edmonton, Alberta
Smed, John – Calgary, Alberta
Smeele, Stan J. – Victoria, British Columbia
Smiley, Donald – Downsview, Ontario
Smiley, Harold – Enderby, British Columbia
Smiley, Lillian – Salmon Arm, British Columbia
Smith, Anne – Timmins, Ontario
Smith, David P. – Ottawa, Ontario
Smith, Denis – Peterborough, Ontario
Smith, Denis – Toronto, Ontario
Smith, Dolina – Scarborough, Ontario
Smith, Edgar A. – Willowdale, Ontario
Smith, George – Winona, Ontario
Smith, Gery, R. C. – Brockville, Ontario
Smith, Jean M. – Keswick, Ontario
Smith, Lillian & Don – Concord, Ontario
Smith, Marion – Windsor, Ontario
Smith, Zeta – Winona, Ontario
Smoke, Lapierre, Arthur – Willowdale, Ontario
Snook, Earl F. – North Vancouver, British Columbia
The Social Credit Party of Alberta – Alberta
Social Credit Party of Canada – Montreal, Quebec
Social Planning and Review Council of
    British Columbia – Vancouver, British Columbia
La Société des Acadiens du Nouveau-Brunswick
Société Franco-Manitobaine – Saint-Boniface, Manitoba
Société nationale des Québécois des Cantons – Coaticook,
    Quebec
La Société Saint-Jean Baptiste de la Mauricie –
    Trois-Rivières, Quebec
Société Saint-Jean Baptiste de Montréal – Montreal, Quebec
Société Saint-Jean Baptiste de Québec – Quebec, Quebec

Sœurs de l'Assomption de la Sainte-Vierge de Nicolet –
    Nicolet, Quebec
Les Sœurs de Notre-Dame du Perpétuel Secours – Saint-
    Damien, Bellechasse, Québec
Search, The Society for Education, Action, Research and
    Counselling on Homosexuality – Vancouver,
    British Columbia
Soltermann, J. – Medicine Hat, Alberta
Somcynsky, Thomas – Sherbrooke, Quebec
Sommerville, R. J. – Peterborough, Ontario
South Central Tribal Council – Kamloops, British Columbia
South Okanagan Civil Liberties Society – Penticton,
    British Columbia
Southwestern Ontario Campaign Life – St. George, Ontario
Soward, S. E. – Victoria, British Columbia
Spallumcheen Band – Enderby, British Columbia
Sparks, Ann – Calgary, Alberta
Spinney, Robert E. – Calgary, Alberta
Splane, Richard B. – Ottawa, Ontario
Stallard, Sidney – New Glasgow, Nova Scotia
Stang, Egbert – Saskatoon, Saskatchewan
Stanton, Michael S. – Calgary, Alberta
Steer, Gary – St. Thomas, Ontario
Stelter, Alice, Wayne – Edmonton, Alberta
Stephens, John V. – Toronto, Ontario
Stevenson, J. G. A. – North Bay, Ontario
Stevenson, S. – London, Ontario
Stewart, E. – Calgary, Alberta
Summer, Audrey – Maple Ridge, British Columbia
Sumpton, James M. – Vancouver, British Columbia
Surrey-White Rock Right to Choose Society –
    Surrey-White Rock, British Columbia
Swift, W. H. – Edmonton, Alberta

T
Tafel, R. D. – North Bay, Ontario
Tait, Janice – Ottawa, Ontario
Tait, Lyal – Port Burwell, Ontario
Tanguay, André – Oshawa, Ontario
Tates, Irene – Kamloops, British Columbia
Taylor, James C. – Toronto, Ontario
Teme-Augama Anishnaboi – Lake Temagami, Ontario
The Poet, John – Chatham, Ontario
Tennant, W. – Kamloops, British Columbia
Tholenau, Carol – Calgary, Alberta
Thomas, Dale – Thamesville, Ontario
Thomas, Eugene – Toronto, Ontario
Thompson, Andrew – Vancouver, British Columbia
Thompson, Cara M. – Barrie, Ontario
Thompson, Daniel L. – St. John's, Newfoundland
Thompson, Edith – Richmond, British Columbia
Thompson, Ruby M. – Wolfville, Nova Scotia

Thunder Bay Multicultural Association – Thunder Bay,
Ontario
Tiffin, V. R. – Victoria, British Columbia
Timmer, F. J. – Kitchener, Ontario
Timmins, Edward & Colleen – Pickering, Ontario
Todres, Irving – Montreal, Quebec
Tomar, Mukhtyae S. – Dartmouth, Nova Scotia
Toosey Band – Williams Lake, British Columbia
Tophom, Reg & Barb – Powassan, Ontario
Toporoski, R. M. – Toronto, Ontario
Torok, Stephen – Timmins, Ontario
The Toronto and Montreal Committee to Defend Quebec's
Right to Self-Determination – Mississauga, Ontario
The Toronto Elizabeth Fry Society – Toronto, Ontario
Tremblay, D. M. – London, Ontario
Tremblay, Peter A. – Sardis, British Columbia
Trethewey, A. – Kingston, Ontario
Trittler, Mauria – St. Thomas, Ontario
Trottier, Colette – St. Thomas, Ontario
Turnbull, M. – Calgary, Alberta
Turner, Jim – Prince Albert, Saskatchewan

U
Ukrainian Canadian Committee – Winnipeg, Manitoba
Ukrainian Greek Orthodox Church of Canada – Edmonton,
Alberta
L'Union culturelle des franco-ontariennes – L'Orignal,
Ontario
Union of British Columbia Indian Chiefs – Vancouver, British
Columbia
Union of British Columbia Municipalities – New Westmin-
ster, British Columbia
Union nationale – Quebec, Quebec
Union of New Brunswick Indians – Fredericton,
New Brunswick
Union of Nova Scotia Indians – Sydney, Nova Scotia
The Union of Ontario Indians – Toronto, Ontario
Union populaire – Charlesbourg, Quebec
United Church of Canada – Edmonton, Alberta
United Church of Canada – Montreal, Quebec
United Church of Canada – St. John's, Newfoundland
United Church of Canada – Truro, Nova Scotia
United Church of Canada – Toronto, Ontario
United Church of Canada – Welland, Ontario
United Hungarian Fund – Toronto, Ontario
United Native Nations Society – Vancouver, British Columbia
The University Women's Club of Barrie – Barrie, Ontario
The University of British Columbia (Members of History
420): Doug, Archer; Hayward, Ann; Braisto, Colin; Keelan,
Mark; Gee, Richard; Leonard, Sandra; Greenword, F. M.;
Seidl, Peter; Wolf, Murray – Vancouver, British Columbia

The University Women's Club of North York – Toronto,
Ontario
The University Women's Club of White Rock – White Rock,
British Columbia
Upper Nicola Indian Band – Merritt, British Columbia
Usher, Dan – Kingston, Ontario

V

Vancouver Community Legal Assistance Society – Vancouver,
British Columbia
The Vancouver Multicultural Society – Vancouver,
British Columbia
Vancouver Quadra Progressive Conservative Association –
Vancouver, British Columbia
Vancouver Status of Women – Vancouver, British Columbia
Van Dom, Gerald – Mississauga, Ontario
Vanden, Bernard E. – Ottawa, Ontario
Vanderwood, Sandra & Jack – Okanagan, British Columbia
Van dev Wal Hylke – Via La Loche, Saskatchewan
Van Dusen, John – Weston, Ontario
Van Koughnet, Edward – Kinsington, Prince Edward Island
Van Mierlo, J. B. – Powassan, Ontario
Vasa Order of American Grand Lodge – Edmonton, Alberta
Verrall, Catherine – Hamilton, Ontario
Verreau, David, Albert, John – Edmonton, Alberta
Vickers, Herb – Calgary, Alberta
Ville de Saint-Nicolas – Saint-Nicolas, Comté de Lévis,
Québec
Voelker, Erwin – Chomedy/Laval, Quebec
Voice for Life – Wingham, Ontario
Voice of Women – Toronto, Ontario
Voluntary Resource Council – Charlottetown,
Prince Edward Island

W

Woechter, Len – Walkerton, Ontario
Wagner, Frank – Toronto, Ontario
Walker, H. K. – Guelph, Ontario
Walker, Marjorie E. – Guelph, Ontario
Walker, Reagan D. – Mississauga, Ontario
Wallace, Donald C. – Downsview, Ontario
Walsh, James F. – St. John's, Newfoundland
Warby, Marney – Hamilton, Ontario
Wardle, Thomas A. – Toronto, Ontario
Warner, J. E. – Hamilton, Ontario
Wasteneys, Geoffrey – Ottawa, Ontario
Waterloo Chronicle – Waterloo, Ontario
Watson, Geoffrey – Picton, Ontario
Watson, John R. – North Battleford, Saskatchewan
Watt, Leonard, J. – Calgary, Alberta
Wawryshyn, Michael – Toronto, Ontario
Way, J. (Mr. & Mrs.) – Powassan, Ontario

Weaver, Monna – Vancouver, British Columbia
Webb, George – Ilderton, Ontario
Weber, Milton – Vancouver, British Columbia
Weidinger, Regince – Cambridge, Ontario
Weiss, Dan – Formosa, Ontario
Wendland, Jack – Maryhill, Ontario
Westbury, Richard S. – Calgary, Alberta
Western Federation Society – Victoria, British Columbia
West Fed Association of Alberta – Edmonton, Alberta
Wettlaufer, Bernice – Weston, Ontario
Weygang, Peter – Kenora, Ontario
Whitby, Percy – Sudbury, Ontario
White, Frank – Victoria, British Columbia
White Rock University Women – Surrey, British Columbia
Wicklum, Earle L. – Weston, Ontario
Wilbur, Keith – Windsor, Ontario
Wildfong, Marjorie – Cambridge, Ontario
Wildsmith, Bruce H. – Halifax, Nova Scotia
Willems, Frank – North Battleford, Saskatchewan
Williams, B. M. – Dartmouth, Nova Scotia
Williams, Paul W. – Ladysmith, British Columbia
Williams, Peter H. – Toronto, Ontario
Williams, Richard – Chilliwack, British Columbia
Williams, S. A. – Ottawa, Ontario
Willis, S. D. – Alliston, Ontario
Wilson, Sam – Cayaga, Ontario
Winslow, Edward T. – West Vancouver, British Columbia
Winsor, William D. – St. John's, Newfoundland
Witchell, John B. – Pierrefonds, Quebec
Wittke, Millie – Eganville, Ontario
Wodiuk, William – Toronto, Ontario
Woehrling, José – Montreal, Quebec
Woledge, Jack O. – Jasper, Alberta
Women's Action Committee for Human Rights – Kitchener, Ontario
Women's Habitat – Etobicoke, Ontario
Women's Research Centre – Vancouver, British Columbia
Women for Political Action – Toronto, Ontario
Wood, Sharon – Alderson, Ontario
Woods, George Beatty – Don Mills, Ontario
Woodward, Helen E. – Mississauga, Ontario
Wright, Bill – Calgary, Alberta
Wright, Cathryn – Wallaceburg, Ontario
Wright, Gerald K. – Duncan, British Columbia
Wright, N. A. – Weston, Ontario
Wyman, Max – Edmonton, Alberta
Wyme, J. C. – Calgary, Alberta
Wynne, Hildburg S. – Ottawa, Ontario